W9-DAA-641

DATE DUE

IDENTIFYING

i

WOOD

The new compact study guide and identifier

WOOD

The new compact study guide and identifier

Aidan Walker

CHARTWELL
BOOKS, INC.

A QUINTET BOOK

Published by Chartwell Books
A Division of Book Sales, Inc.
114 Northfield Avenue
Edison, New Jersey 08837

This edition produced for sale
in the USA, its territories
and dependencies only.

ISBN 0-7858-0777-2

This book was designed and produced by
Quintet Publishing Limited
6 Blundell Street
London N7 9BH

Creative Director: Richard Dewing
Designer: James Lawrence
Project Editor: Kathy Steer
Editor: Andrew Armitage
Photographer: Keith Waterton

Typeset in Great Britain by
Central Southern Typesetters, Eastbourne
Manufactured in Singapore by
Bright Arts Pte Ltd.
Printed in China by
Leefung-Asco Printers Ltd.

Acknowledgements

The material in this publication previously appeared in:
The Encyclopedia of Wood by Aidan Walker.
Photography on pages 16(t), 18, 19(b), 21(b), 22(t), 28(t),
31(b), 32(b), 40(b), 42(t), 44(b), 45(t), 46(t), 47(b), 48(b), 49,
50(b), 56(b), 59(b), 61(t), 62(b), 65(b), 71(t), 75, 78(t)
courtesy of Ken Southall, Member of U.K. Branch of
International Wood Collector's Society

International Wood Collector's Society
Bill Cockrell, 2300 West Range Line Road,
Greencastle IN 46135-9574.
While every effort has been made to trace and
acknowledge all copyright holders, we would like to
apologise should any omissions have been made.

CONTENTS

INTRODUCTION

ABOVE: This unusual bowl has been carved out of one piece of wood.

Of all the materials that enhance our lives, wood is perhaps the only one that appeals to all five senses. It is delightful to look at, either in its natural state or in the form of a stunning artifact – whether bole or bowl, so to speak. It is often used for its aromatic properties. It is "heard" when used in musical instruments. The work of the artist or artisan is often sensual to the touch. And taste may not be immediately obvious as an attribute of wood – until you consider that wines, spirits, sauces, and other foodstuffs are often matured in wooden casks.

The heart of this **Identifier** book is its **Wood identifying section** on pages 15–79. This gives information on 130 different types of wood, and they are listed in alphabetical order according to their Latin name. Woods go by various popular names, but each has only one Latin name. Popular names, however, are to be found in the **Index** on page 80.

With each entry, information has been provided not only in words but also in a graphical, tabular form, which will enable you to see at a glance how good a particular type of wood is for your purposes – whether you are making fine furniture, works of art, or a tree house, or are simply interested in wood.

This book will help you to make choices that are right for you, your work, and your environment.

THE WORLD OF WOOD

A world without wood would be unthinkable. From early shelter, implements, and weapons, through seafaring vessels and transport old and new to modern buildings, art, and artifacts, wood has been essential to humankind. And that doesn't even take into account its sheer beauty in its natural state and the habitat it provides for countless species of flora and fauna.

An equally important function of wood is its role with the oceans as the lungs of our planet and, through its own rhythms of take-up and release of moisture, the vital part it plays in regulating our climate.

Wood holds such a place in our culture — the cultures of *all* peoples on Planet Earth — that there's little wonder that many believe trees house spirits. Much folklore surrounds wood: There's the sacred ash tree called Yggdrasil, central to a potent legend in Norse mythology; and the belief among the Greeks of old, who said nymphs would plant elms in remembrance of fallen heroes. Trees have the longest lifespan of all forms of life. The oldest survivor is a Bristlecone pine (*Pinus longeava*), which grows in the White Mountains of California, is at least 5,000 years old, and was probably a seedling when the Egyptians built their pyramids. Trees are also the heaviest living things.

Conifers, which we call softwoods, emerged 275 million years ago, eventually covering two-thirds of the earth's surface. The broad-leaved, flowering, and fruit-bearing hardwood trees first emerged about 140 million years after the conifers. The conifers provide the bulk of the world's lumber.

ABOVE: This chair is a very dramatic and striking design carved out of bleached oak.

GRAIN, FIGURE, AND ODOR

ABOVE: Another fine example of utilising wood.

We are all familiar with a tree's growth rings. As the sap rises in the spring and stops in the fall in temperate climates, this interrupted growth cycle causes a distinctive wood layer to form, and this is called a growth ring. These are not really "annual rings" by which to count the age of a tree, because cold winters or periodic droughts can interrupt the growth cycle. In the tropics the growth may be continuous, and the wood may appear to have no growth rings at all.

Each growth ring has two distinct zones. Fast-growing earlywood cells formed in the spring have thin walls and large cavities, while slower-growing latewood cells formed in the summer have small cavities with thick walls. It is the contrast between these two layers that enables us to identify the tree with the naked eye, when viewing an end section.

When you say a piece of wood has a beautiful grain, you are more likely to be talking about the surface pattern on a cross section of the trunk, also known as the wood's "figure." Grain, strictly speaking, refers to the lines visible on a cut board that show the intersection of the growth rings and the plane of the board itself.

The natural arrangement of the wood fibers in relation to the main axis of the tree produces several types of grain. Crossgrain, appears when the fibers are not parallel to the main axis of the tree, and wavy grain where the fibers form short waves in a regular pattern. You can also find curly grain and spiral grain, diagonal grain and interlocked grain.

Texture is governed by the variation in size of the early – and latewood cells. There's also the quality of luster – which

THE WORLD OF WOOD

*ABOVE: A contemporary-style desk
and matching stool.*

is the ability of the wood cells to reflect light, and this is related to texture. Smooth, fine-textured woods are more lustrous than course-textured ones.

Then there's odor. Resinous pines and many other woods have a strong natural odor. One such is camphorwood, which is used to line the interior of closets; another is cigar-box cedar, which is used to make humidifiers.

THE WORLD'S FORESTS

Coniferous forests can grow from just below the polar regions, through temperate latitudes, right into areas of Mediterranean climate. They can also grow in temperate climate. The southern pines of the USA survive the winter by restricting water loss through their very long and tough, narrow, needle-shaped leaves with blue waxy surfaces.

Temperate hardwood forests are broad-leaved forests that stretch across the temperate zones of America, Europe, and Asia. Oak, beech, ash, birch, and what Americans call sugar maple – while the British call it maple – occur in pure or mixed stands in the most northern regions.

Mediterranean forests lie to the south of the temperate region, and are mixed forests of conifers and broad-leaved evergreen trees.

Sub-tropical forests grow below the temperate zones, and there are the sub-tropical forests of Central and South America, Europe, Central and West Africa, India, Asia, South Africa, and Southern and Western Australia. Each area has its own characteristic forest types, designed to resist summer drought rather than winter cold.

Savannah forests occur in North America, where there is heavy rainfall: on the open prairies of Canada, east of the Rockies, and on the plains of the United States as far south as the Gulf of Mexico. Almost a third of the land surface of the world is arid, with high daytime temperatures and very cold nighttime temperatures. Not all these desert areas are flat: some are mountainous, such as the Painted Desert in the USA.

Tropical rainforests occur in South America, West, Central, and East Africa, and from India, Malaysia and Indonesia throughout South-East Asia to Papua New Guinea. It's lush forest, beautiful and essential to the earth's ecosystem. There's an extraordinary variety of trees, hundreds of different species per square kilometer (or about half a square mile).

Mixed hardwood and coniferous forests occur in the Northern Temperate zone. Further north, coniferous trees predominate and conversely there are more hardwood trees in the southern areas.

CONVERSION

Before wood can be used, it has to be transformed from its raw lumber form into "dimensioned" form. This process is known as conversion. It is a process that usually comprises cutting, grading, seasoning, and preserving.

Lumber is usually cut to maximize the yield of planks. The way it is cut will not only determine how much usable wood you can get from a log, but also how the resultant wood will release and absorb moisture, and therefore how it shrinks and expands as it does so.

Flat-sawn wood is less economical. It produces the widest but least stable boards. Radial sawing will be less economical but produce greater dimensional stability.

Lumber is graded according to the use it will be put to. In the case of furniture, appearance will take precedence, while strength will be more highly prized in, say, constructional use.

Wood is hygroscopic. That is to say it picks up moisture, and will experience internal "movement" as it dries. Seasoning, therefore, is important if that phenomenon is to be minimized.

Air drying is the traditional method of reducing moisture content. This is done by maximizing the drying effect of the wind while minimizing the effects of the windblown rain and fog. This system is used with varying degrees of success depending on the climate, of course, and in some wetter climates is often used only as a pre-drying process prior to treating with preservatives and kilning.

Kiln drying, especially in bulk, is usually the preserve of professional dryers. Lumber is stacked, often with smaller pieces of softwood placed between the planks, to give support and allow air to flow evenly. Kilns are sealed and the temperature and humidity are monitored, as well as the duration of kilning. Too fast a drying process can be as disastrous as one that's too slow.

Preservation extends the life of wood, providing a protective "shell." Some woods have a natural resistance to insect attack and decay. Cedar is one such: it is resistant to termite attack and is normally unaffected by woodworm. These naturally durable woods can last for a few years to several centuries, depending on the degree of exposure.

There are three main types of preservative. Tar oils such as the traditional creosote are used mainly on fences and outbuildings. Its oily nature slows weathering. Water borne preservatives are applied by vacuum/pressure impregnation, and this process fixes the most common copper-chrome-arsenic types as insoluble in the wood, giving high levels of protection. Then there are organic solvent-borne preservatives, again applied by vacuum/pressure techniques or by dip. Brushing provides only minimal protection.

LEFT: This elegant chair carved out of cherry can be easily made using beech.

Nineteen Favorite Woods

ere are brief outlines of 19 of the best-known woods used today. Some, while beautiful, should be bought with care, in case they are not from a sustainable source.

ASH has flexibility, strength and reliability, was invaluable for military use – lances, spears, pikes, and javelins were made from it since before the Bronze Age to the late 18th century. Good for shock absorbency, and able to with-stand repeated impact without fracturing.

BEECH may warp if carelessly dried. This tree has not been highly esteemed by cabinet-makers. Today it is used for production of cellulose and artificial fibers. Used where required sections are small and movement is less important: chair spindles and upholstery frames.

BOX is one of the densest woods and is used for small items like chessmen, corkscrews, and snuff boxes. It was the art of the engraver that flourished with box, from the 15th century, right to the 1920s.

CEDAR is the name applied to over 70 different kinds of wood, most of them evergreen. Favored for being light and workable in sturdy sections. Noted for its resistance to termite attack, normally unaffected by woodworm.

DEAL has been the collective name for larch, spruce and pine since the 14th century – but it now describes the con-verted timbers of coniferous softwoods. These are unbeat-able for straightness, strength and economy, and all conifer-ous softwoods contribute to America's characteristic house architecture.

EBONY is a trade name given to species of *Diospyros*, which have black heartwood, in contrast, to the North American white ebony, known as persimmon.

ELM was decimated by Dutch Elm disease, a virulent strain of which went from Canada to Europe in the late 1960s and altered the landscape by killing off its heroic hedgerow trees. A strong, swirling figure gives a sensuous appearance to the polished wood, and it has been exploited by modern sculptors. It tends to warp and crack, and can be awkward to work with hand tools.

EUCALYPTUS is the name given to a genus of trees indigenous to Australia and Tasmania. It's been introduced to various parts of the world, and does well in California and South Africa. Its leaf glands contain volatile aromatic oil, used as an expectorant.

FRUITWOOD especially apple, cherry, and pear, is favored by craftsmen. Rurally manufactured furniture can be found either made from these woods or decorated with inlays using them. Cherry has been used as a cabinet wood in America and Britain because of its resemblance to mahogany.

HAZEL AND WILLOW

From willow comes salicylic acid, the principal ingredient of aspirin, and was known to the Romans for its power to relieve pain. It holds up well when submerged. Hazel is thin, soft and pliable, but not especially durable. Used for spars, sheep hurdles, cask hoops and basketwork.

LIGNUM VITAE The best of this hard wood comes from the West Indies, coastal regions of Colombia and Venezuela, and from Central America. Not favored as a cabinet wood because the trees are narrow and short. It *is* valued for its weight, density, and toughness.

LIME is visually striking, and noted for its longevity. It's a soft hardwood, close-grained and creamy, and easily worked. Popular with carvers, who, in the Middle Ages, called it "sacrum lignum" – the holy wood – because they associated it with the figures of Christ, the Virgin, and the Apostles.

MAHOGANY was first mentioned in furniture advertisements in South Carolina in 1730 – when Thomas Chippendale founded his company. It's light, strong, and versatile, and suited to the thin sections of latticework in music stands and chair backs. Early names include Baywood (after the Bay of Honduras) and Havana wood.

OAK (*Quercus robor* from which comes the word "robust") is associated with the history of Britain. It's renowned for its strength, durability, and vitality. Used for lock gates (before greenheart), timber-frame houses, and wheel spokes.

ROSEWOOD has nothing to do with roses, but the name comes from the supposedly fragrant scent of the timber. Cousins include pinkwood (called tulipwood outside the USA), kingwood and cocobolo. Seldom seen in the solid.

SYCAMORE AND MAPLE

What the Americans call maple, the British call sycamore, and what the Americans call sycamore, the British call lacewood. These woods, are crisp and creamy white, sometimes with distinctive figure, arising from irregular growth.

TEAK conjures up images of elephants, sampans, and straw hats. It's one of the hardest, strongest, and most durable of woods – so hard that it was customary in the 19th century for European cabinetmakers to demand extra payment when converting this wood into furniture, to compensate for blunting their tools!

WALNUT is a native of central Asia, but the native American species is known as Virginia walnut, and was first planted in England as early as 1656. It is darker, straighter, seldom as finely figured, but has many similar properties as the other species. A tree as much loved for the products of its branches as for its exceptional wood.

YEW's evergreen leaves have since ancient times been held to symbolize everlasting life. Although one of the hardest woods of all, it is classified as a softwood. Very popular for smaller items, such as snuff- and pillboxes, because its trunks tend to be deeply fluted and twisted, making conversion into planks uneconomical and impractical.

THE RAINFORESTS

The rainforest covers about 3½ million square miles – 7% of the earth's land surface. Researchers say 50% of the existing rainforest has been lost since the beginning of the century – probably even more.

Some of these forests have existed in much the same form for millions of years, and this long history has ensured their extraordinary diversity. It is frightening to think of the speed at which the remaining forest is being removed – sometimes, as in the Amazon, burned to create large impoverished grasslands for short-term beef production for export to the USA.

On the world scale, some researchers have put destruction of the rainforest at 100 acres *per minute*. That's a lot of trees, and a lot of habitat – not to mention the effect on the wider ecosystem. Witness the greenhouse effect – the gradual warming of the atmosphere caused by a build-up of carbon dioxide, which traps the sun's heat. When the vast forests become contributors to that build-up, that is, by being burned rather than allowed to play their natural role of consuming the gas, the ecological implications are dire.

The key to the future of the forests' survival is the possibility of sustainable lumber yield through efficient forest management. It is vitally necessary to change policies of short-term gain into those of long-term forest management.

You can help this process in your choice of materials that you buy. The scarcity or otherwise of any particular type of wood will change, depending on how it is being harvested at any given point in time. It would be impractical, therefore, for a book that may be on your shelf for several years to prescribe and proscribe. But you should check with your supplier or local environmental group if you are unsure about the wood.

WOOD IDENTIFIER

Each of the following entries has a colored side bar, which marks out of ten the most important characteristics of each wood.

Impact bending: This shows the wood's resistance to suddenly applied loads – a measure of its toughness.

Stiffness: A measure of the elasticity of the wood, to be considered in conjunction with the bending strength. Important for wood that's going to be used as a long column or strut.

Density: Is measured as specific gravity, the ratio of the density of a substance to that of water.

Workability: This shows how easily a wood is worked and whether it has a significant blunting effect on tools.

Bending strength – also known as the maximum bending strength. This is tested by applying pressure to the end of a board until it cracks.

Crushing strength is the wood's ability to withstand loads applied to the end grain – a critical test for wood that's going to be used as short columns or props.

This indicates whether the tree is a hardwood or softwood.

H	S
HARDWOOD	SOFTWOOD

NOTE: What's known as maple in the USA is known as sycamore in the UK. Similarly, what Americans call sugar maple, the British call maple. In Australia, oak, ash, and elm are entirely different species from those recognized in the USA and Europe. There's an international code of botanical nomenclature, using Latin names, by which categories of flora and fauna can be recognized the world over.

ABIES SPP. *FAMILY:* PINACEAE

Silver Fir *(whitewood)*

Where it grows
Only the *Abies* spp. produce true fir trees. *A. lasiocarpa* produces alpine fir, which occurs from Alaska to New Mexico. *A. procera* provides noble fir from the Western USA. Silver fir grows extensively in Britain and mid-Europe.

Appearance
Color varies from creamy-white to pale yellow-brown, closely resembling European spruce, but is slightly less lustrous. The wood is straight-grained with a fine texture.

Properties
Slightly resinous weighing about 30 lb/ft^3 when dry. There is medium movement in service; it has low stiffness and resistance to shock loads, with medium bending and crushing strengths, but poor steam-bending rating.

Workability
Works well with both hand and machine tools and has little dulling effect on cutters if they're kept reasonably sharp.

Preservation
Subject to damage by pinhole borer, longhorn and Buprestid beetles; is non-durable and moderately resistant to preservative. The sapwood is permeable.

Uses
Building work, carcassing, interior construction, carpentry, boxes, pallets, and crates. Small trees are used in the round for scaffolding and poles.

ACER PSEUDOPLATANUS *FAMILY:* ACERACEAE

Maple *(USA)/*Sycamore *(UK)*

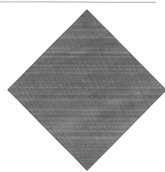

Where it grows
A native of central and southern Europe and western Asia, it grows in varying soil and exposure conditions in the UK. It is known as sycamore plane, great maple (England) or plane (Scotland). Field maple and Norway maple are similar and both grow in Europe.

Appearance
A creamy-white color with a natural luster. If slowly dried, it turns to a light tan. Usually straight-grained, but curly or wavy grain produces attractive "fiddleback" or lace-ray figure on quartered surfaces. The texture is fine and even.

Properties
Medium density (about 38 lb/ft^3). It air-dries rapidly but may stain unless end-stacked. Has medium movement in service, medium bending and crushing strength, low shock resistance and very low stiffness, so has good steam-bending properties.

Workability
Moderate blunting effect on tools and cutting edges. The grain tends to pick up when planing or molding interlocked or wavy grain on quartered stock, so a reduction of the cutting angle is recommended.

Preservation
Sapwood is liable to attack by the common furniture beetle and by *Ptilinus pectinicornis*.

Uses
Fingerboards and ribs of lutes, violin backs. Good turnery wood for brush handles and domestic utensils, and selected logs are sliced to produce attractive figure for cabinets and paneling.

ACER SPP. *FAMILY:* ACERACEAE

Soft Maple

Where it grows
More than 10 species of this genus grow in north temperate regions of Canada and the eastern USA and on the Pacific coast, but only about five are important lumber sources.

Appearance
Creamy-white with a close, straight grain and indistinct growth rings on plain-sawn surfaces. Even texture,
fine and slightly less lustrous than rock maple, and lighter in weight.

Properties
A. rubrum weighs about 38 lb/ft^3, while A. saccharinum and A. macrophyllum are 34 lb/ft^3. Dries slowly with little degrade, and medium movement in service. Soft maple is of medium density with good bending and crushing strengths and low stiffness and shock resistance.

Workability
Works well with both hand and machine tools, offering only a moderate blunting effect. Nail and screw with care.

Preservation
Moderately resistant to preservation treatment; the sapwood is liable to insect attack but is permeable.

Uses
Suitable for furniture, interior joinery, turnery and domestic woodware. Specialized uses include sports goods, dairy and laundry equipment, musical instruments, and piano actions. Can be sliced to produce figured veneers for cabinets etc.

3
3
6
6
6.
6
H

ACER SACCHARUM *FAMILY:* ACERACEAE

Rock Maple/Sugar Maple

Where it grows
This and A. nigrum are known as hard maple in the USA, Canada, and the UK. Sap from the sugar maple is processed into maple sugar and syrup. One of the most valuable woods growing east of the Rockies, and in the northern and eastern States.

Appearance
Creamy-white with a reddish tinge, sometimes with a dark-brown heart. Usually straight-grained but often curly or wavy, with fine brown lines marking the growth rings on plain-sawn surfaces. An even texture, fine and lustrous.

Properties
It weighs 45 lb/ft^3 and dries fairly slowly with little degrade. There's medium movement in service. It has medium density with good bending and crushing strengths, low stiffness and shock resistance, and a good steam-bending rating.

Workability
Tends to ride on cutters and burn during endgrain working. Needs pre-boring for nailing but glues well.

Preservation
Liable to beetle attack and growth defects caused by insects. Heartwood is resistant to preservation but sapwood is permeable.

Uses
Industrial flooring, roller-skating rinks, dance halls, butchers' blocks, piano actions and sports goods. A valuable turnery wood.

8
6
8
6
8
9
H

ACER SACCHARUM *FAMILY:* ACERACEAE

Birds-Eye Maple

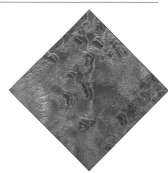

Where it grows
The characteristic figure in birds-eye maple is a fairly rare occurrence, making it a highly prized timber. There is no satisfactory explanation as to why this special grain figure only appears in a few trees, sometimes growing alongside other plain figured trees. It is found growing at its best in regions from Nova Scotia westwards to Ontario and then the North and Eastern United States.

Appearance
White or creamy-white in color sometimes with a reddish or brownish heartwood. Usually with a uniform texture and a straight fine grain. The density and size of the individual "birds-eyes" vary greatly from tree to tree and different parts of the same tree.

Properties
With a weight of 47lb/ft^3 it dries rather slowly with a considerable amount of shrinkage. There is medium movement in service. It has medium density.

Workability
Care needs to be taken to avoid the "birds-eyes" tearing out during planing operations. There is a tendency for the timber to leave burn marks when circular sawing.

Preservation
The timber is non-durable, being liable to attack by the furniture beetle. The heartwood is resistant to preservatives whilst the sapwood is permeable.

Uses
High class furniture is made with this timber although the vast majority of timber processed is made into veneers for furniture and paneling.

AESCULUS HIPPOCASTANUM *FAMILY:* HIPPOCASTANACEAE

Horse Chestnut

Where it grows
Native to Albania, it thrives in the mountain regions of northern Greece, Bulgaria, Iran, and northern India, and is now widespread throughout North America and Europe. Called buckeye in North America because the base of the nuts resemble the eyes of a deer.

Appearance
Very white when felled in early winter, but pale yellow-brown if felled later in the year. Spiral grain is usually present, and the wood is inclined to be cross- or wavy-grained. Has a very fine, close, uniform texture.

Properties
Weighs about 32 lb/ft^3 and dries well with little degrade and with small movement in service. Has low bending strength, very low stiffness, and low-to-medium crushing strength, with a good steam-bending classification.

Workability
Worked easily with hand and machine tools with only slight blunting. Nailing and screwing are satisfactory, and it glues well and gives a good finish when stained and polished.

Preservation
Liable to attack by the common furniture beetle, but is permeable to preservation treatment.

Uses
Furniture and carving, turnery; handpieces for tennis rackets. Selected logs are sliced for handsome veneers.

AGATHIS SPP. *FAMILY:* ARAUCARIACEAE

Kauri Pine

darker in color and coarser in texture. Heartwood varies from pale cookie to pink or even dark red-brown. Has a fine texture and a lustrous surface.

Properties

New Zealand kauri weighs 36 lb/ft^3, while Queensland kauri is 30 lb/ft^3. Dries at a moderate rate with a tendency to warp, but is stable in use. Has high stiffness, medium bending and crushing strength and resistance to shock, but is not suitable for steam-bending.

Workability

Works easily with hand and machine tools, with only a slight dulling effect on edges. In boring or mortising it needs to be properly supported at the tool exit. Holds nails and screws well.

Preservation

Subject to attack by the common furniture beetle, but is moderately durable and resistant to preservation treatment.

Uses

Vats, wooden machinery, boats and building. Queensland and Fiji kauri are used for high-class joinery and cabinet work.

Where it grows

These cone-bearing softwoods occur singly or in small groves intermingled with broad-leaved trees, and are distributed from Malaysia to Australia, from New Guinea to New Zealand and Fiji.

Appearance

Straight-grained and valuable, these woods are not true pines, resembling the botanically related "parana pine" in appearance, but

---

ALNUS GLUTINOSA *FAMILY:* BETULACEAE

Common Alder

Appearance

Both sapwood and heartwood are a dull, lusterless, bright orange-brown when freshly cut, maturing to light reddish-brown with darker lines. A fine-textured wood, and straight grained, except near the butts.

Properties

Dries quickly and is of medium density (about 33 lb/ft^3). Has a low bending strength and shock resistance, a medium crushing strength and very low stiffness, which earns it a moderate steam-bending rating.

Workability

Can be machined easily if cutting edges are kept sharp, with only slight blunting. Nailing and screw-holding are satisfactory, and will stain and polish to a good finish.

Preservation

The sapwood is liable to attack by the common furniture beetle. The wood is perishable but permeable for preservation treatment.

Uses

Carving, turnery, domestic woodware, broom handles, wooden toys, artificial limbs. Can be sliced for veneers.

Where it grows

A native to Europe and North Africa, but has a wide distribution throughout the northern hemisphere. Red alder is one of the most common commercial hardwoods and is widely distributed on the Pacific coast of Canada and the USA.

ANISOPTERA SPP. *FAMILY:* DIPTEROCARPACEAE

Mersawa and Krabak

Where it grows
There are many species of the genus *Anisoptera*, usually mixed in the countries of origin and exported in a group under the trade names of mersawa or krabak. Found in Malaya, Sabah, Brunei, Sarawak, Thailand, Burma, and the Philippines.

Appearance
The sapwood is usually attacked by a blue fungus, which stains it. The heartwood varies from pale yellow to yellow-brown, with a pink tinge, and is moderately coarse but even in texture. Grain varies from straight to interlocked.

Properties
Weight averages 40 lb/ft^3. Dries very slowly from green. Has a low bending strength and shock resistance, with medium crushing strength. Has very low stiffness and a poor steam-bending rating.

Workability
Interlocked grain and silica content causes severe blunting of edges. Can be nailed and glued easily and brought to a good finish.

Preservation
The sapwood is liable to attack by the powder post beetle. The wood is moderately durable and resistant to preservation treatment.

Uses
Furniture, general construction, interior joinery, flooring, vehicle bodies, planking for boats. It is rotary-cut for utility plywood, and sliced for veneers. Check with your local environmental group before buying.

ARAUCARIA ANGUSTIFOLIA *FAMILY:* ARAUCARIACEAE

Parana Pine

Where it grows
Mainly in the Brazilian state of Parana, and is also found in Paraguay and northern Argentina. Is also known in the USA as Brazilian pine, and is closely related to the so-called Chile pine or Monkeypuzzle tree.

Appearance
Very close density, almost complete absence of growth rings, and unusual coloring make it a very attractive wood. Mainly straight-grained and honey-colored, although dark gray patches appear at the inner core of the heartwood.

Properties
Weight varies between 30-40 lb/ft^3. Not durable, and has only medium bending and crushing strengths, with low resistance to shock. Very difficult to dry, showing a tendency to split in the darker areas. Can distort alarmingly if not well dried.

Workability
Good with both hand and machine tools, and planes and molds cleanly and to a smooth finish.

Preservation
Liable to attack by the pinhole borer beetle and common furniture beetle. Is non-durable and moderately resistant to preservation treatment, but the sapwood is permeable for preservation treatment.

Uses
Internal joinery, especially staircases; also cabinet framing, store fitting and vehicle building. Check with your local environmental group or supplier before buying.

AUCOUMEA KLAINEANA *FAMILY:* BURSERACEAE

Gaboon

Where it grows
This wood – which is exported more than any other African wood – grows mostly In Equatorial Guinea, Gabon and the Congo Republic.

Appearance
The heartwood is light pink, pink-brown on exposure. Commonly straight-grained and sometimes shallowly interlocked or slightly wavy, giving an attractive stripe on quartered surfaces. It has a medium, uniform texture with a natural luster.

Properties
A weak, light wood (23-35 lb/ft^3; averages around 27 lb/ft^3). Dries rapidly with little degrade, and there's medium movement in service. Has low bending strength, very low stiffness, medium crushing strength, and a poor steam-bending rating. Not very durable or resistant to decay.

Workability
Works fairly well with hand and machine tools, but is rather woolly with moderately severe blunting of edges. Grain tends to pick up when planing or molding irregular grain on quartered surfaces. Nails without difficulty and glues easily.

Preservation
Sapwood is liable to attack by the powder post beetle. The wood is non-durable and resistant to preservation treatment.

Uses
Plywood, blockboard and laminboard, which are used for a variety of purposes. Check with your local environmental group or supplier before buying.

BETULA PAPYRIFERA *FAMILY:* BETULACEAE

Paper Birch

Where it grows
Native Americans made their canoes from the bark of this tree. Today it grows from the Yukon to Hudson Bay, and Newfoundland down to the eastern USA. Along with yellow birch, it is known as American birch in the UK, and white birch in Canada.

Appearance
Creamy-white sapwood, pale brown heartwood, normally with a straight grain and fine, uniform texture. Many of the logs produce a curly figure known as "flame" birch. As with yellow birch, it gets pith flecks, which can be an attractive feature.

Properties
Medium-density (39 lb/ft^3). Dries slowly with little degrade. Has medium strength in all categories except stiffness, and has only a moderate steam-bending rating.

Workability
Works fairly well with hand and machine tools, with moderate blunting. Sometimes curly grain may pick up with planing or molding on quartered surfaces, and a reduced cutter angle is recommended.

Preservation
Is non-durable and moderately resistant to preservative treatment, but the sapwood is permeable.

Uses
Mostly rotary cut for plywood; good for turnery; pulped for paper; sliced for veneers.

BETULA PENDULA *FAMILY:* BETULACEAE

European Birch

Where it grows
It endures extremes of cold and heat and can be found further north than any other broad-leaved tree, as far as Lapland. Also grows throughout Europe, and is sold according to its country of origin: Swedish birch, English birch etc.

Appearance
Featureless creamy-white to pale brown. Straight grained and fine-textured. Pith flecks can show as irregular dark markings. Grain deviation causes "flame" and "curly" figure.

Properties
Heavy and dense (41 lb/ft^3). Slight tendency to warp when drying.

Moderately stable in use, with high bending and crushing strengths, medium stiffness and shock resistance. Not good for steam-bending.

Workability
Works easily with hand and machine tools, but may be woolly. Reduced cutter angle is recommended to prevent tearing of irregular-grained material. Pre-bore for nailing or screwing.

Preservation
Sapwood is liable to attack by the common furniture beetle. Heartwood is moderately resistant to preservative treatment but the sapwood is permeable.

Uses
A major material for birch plywood in Finland and former USSR. Solid, it's used for upholstery framing, interior joinery and furniture. Also suitable for turnery.

BUXUS SEMPERVIRENS *FAMILY:* BUXACEAE

European Boxwood

Where it grows
One of the few evergreen broad-leaved trees that occur in mild temperate climates. It grows in the UK, Europe, North Africa, Asia Minor, and western Asia.

Appearance
Pale bright orange-yellow, occasionally straight-grained but often irregular, especially from small trees grown in Britain. Has compact, fine and even texture.

Properties
Weight varies from 52-71 lb/ft^3, averaging 57 lb/ft^3. Dries slowly and may develop surface checks or split badly if dried in the round.

Billets are soaked in a solution of common salt or urea before drying, and end coatings applied. Very dense, hard, and durable with a good steam-bending rating, high stiffness, good crushing strength and resistance to shock.

Workability
Has a high resistance to cutters, which should be kept very sharp to prevent wood from burning when boring or recessing. Irregular grain tends to tear in planing. Pre-bore for nailing and screwing.

Preservation
The sapwood is liable to attack by the common furniture beetle.

Heartwood is durable and resistant to preservative treatment.

Uses
Textile rollers, shuttles, pulley blocks, skittles, croquet mallets, and tool handles. Also in demand for wood sculpture and carving; engraving blocks, parts of musical instruments, chessmen and corkscrews.

CALOPHYLLUM BRASILIENSE *FAMILY:* GUTTIFERAE

Jacareuba

Where it grows

Widely distributed in the tropics, grows throughout the West Indies, and from Southern Mexico down into the northern parts of South America.

Appearance

Heartwood varies from yellow-pink to rich red-brown (with the grain commonly interlocked, often with fine dark red parenchyma stripes), with the indistinct band of yellow sapwood lighter in color. The wood has a fairly uniform, medium texture.

Properties

Weight varies from 34-44 lb/ft^3. It is difficult to air-dry because it dries slowly with a lot of warping and splitting. It has medium bending strength and shock resistance, with low stiffness and high crushing strength. It has a moderate steam-bending rating.

Workability

Moderately easy to machine but the soft parenchyma tissue tends to pick up badly and brown gum streaks can cause rapid blunting.

Reduced cutting angle is recommended, as is pre-boring for screwing and nailing.

Preservation

Very resistant to preservation treatment, but the sapwood is permeable.

Uses

Exterior joinery, general construction, bridge-building, shingles, ship-building and so on. Also for interior construction and joinery. Selected logs are sliced for veneers. Check with your local environmental group or supplier before buying.

CARDWELLIA SUBLIMIS *FAMILY:* PROTEACEAE

Australian Silky Oak

Where it grows

The name "silky oak" – given to a number of different genera and species in Australia and New Zealand – originally referred to *Grevillea robusta*, a native of southern Queensland.

Appearance

Attractive with well-marked ray figure showing on quartered surfaces – but it is not a true oak. Heartwood is pink to reddish-brown, maturing to darker red-brown. But *Cardwellia* is generally darker than that of *Grevillea*, which is a paler pink-brown. Usually straight-grained, except where wood fibers distort.

Properties

Grevillea is about 36 lb/ft^3, while *Cardwellia* is about 34 lb/ft^3. Hard to dry, and given to severe cupping of wide boards. There is medium movement in use, below average strength in all categories relative to its density.

Workability

Works readily with hand and machine tools with only slight blunting. Quarter-sawn material tends to pickup when planing or molding, and a reduced cutting angle is advised. Good nail-holding properties.

Preservation

Sapwood is liable to attack by the powder post beetle. Heartwood is moderately durable and resistant to preservation treatment.

Uses

Building and shuttering; top grades used for furniture, interior joinery, paneling, etc.

CARPINUS BETULUS *FAMILY:* BETULACEAE

Hornbeam

Where it grows
About 20 species grow in European northern temperate zones, from Sweden to Asia Minor, but the commercial species grow in France, Turkey, and Iran.

Appearance
A dull white color marked with gray streaks and flecks caused by the broad ray structure, which gives a flecked figure on quartered surfaces. Usually irregular or cross-grained, but has a fine, even texture.

Properties
Weighs on average 47 lb/ft³. Dries fairly quickly and well with little degrade, but much movement in service. Heavy and dense with a high bending and crushing strength, medium stiffness and resistance to shock, and good shear strength and resistance to splitting, with a good steam-bending rating.

Workability
Difficult to work, with a high resistance to cutting, with moderate blunting. Finishes smoothly, glues well, takes stain and polish and takes an excellent finish.

Preservation
Sapwood is liable to attack by the common furniture beetle and the heartwood is non-durable but permeable for preservation treatment.

Uses
Good for turnery and used for brushbacks, drumsticks, pool cues, skittles and Indian clubs. Also used for piano actions and other musical instrument parts, and also in flooring.

CARYA SPP. *FAMILY:* JUGLANDACEAE

Hickory

Where it grows
More than 20 species grow in the large forests of eastern Canada and the eastern US, but there are only four commercial species.

Appearance
The sapwood is very pale gray ("white hickory"), preferred to the heartwood, which is red to reddish-brown ("red hickory"). Usually straight-grained but occasionally wavy or irregular, with a rather coarse texture.

Properties
Weight ranges from 45-56 lb/ft³ but averages 51 lb/ft³. It needs careful drying but is stable in service, very dense with high toughness, bending, stiffness, and crushing strengths, and exceptional shock resistance. It has excellent steam-bending properties.

Workability
Difficult to machine, and has moderate blunting effect. Also difficult to glue, but stains and polishes well.

Preservation
Sapwood is liable to attack by the powder post beetle, and the heartwood is moderately resistant to preservation treatment.

Uses
Ideal for handles of striking tools; also for wheel spokes, chairs, and ladder rungs. Valuable for sculpture and carving; also used for sports equipment. Is rotary cut for plywood faces and sliced for veneers.

Where it grows
Native of south-west Europe and grows in Britain, France, Germany, North Africa, and western Asia.

Appearance
Heartwood is straw-to-brown, resembling oak, distinct from the narrow sapwood. The wood has prominent growth rings but fine

CASTANEA SATIVA *FAMILY:* FAGACEAE

Sweet Chestnut

rays. Grain is straight but often spiral, and has a coarse texture.

Properties
Weight averages 34 lb/ft^3. In drying, it retains moisture in patches, and doesn't respond well to kiln reconditioning. Its acidic nature tends to corrode iron fastenings in damp conditions. Has low bending strength, very low stiffness and shock resistance, and medium crushing strength. Air-dried wood has a good bending rating if free from knots.

Workability
Works well with both hand and machine tools, with only slight

blunting. Has good screw and nail holding, glues well, and stains and polishes to an excellent finish.

Preservation
Sapwood is liable to attack by the powder post beetle and common furniture beetle; heartwood is durable and very resistant to preservation treatment.

Uses
Often substituted for oak in furniture; also used for casket boards, domestic woodware, turnery, walking sticks, fencing, and often makes staves for casks for oils, fats, fruit juices, and wines.

Where it grows
This small to medium-sized tree grows in the moist scrub forests of Australia, in New South Wales and Eastern Queensland. It's also known as Moreton Bay bean, Moreton Bay chestnut, and beantree.

Appearance
Heartwood has a chocolate color with narrow gray-brown streaks of

CASTANOSPERMUM AUSTRALE *FAMILY:* LEGUMINOSAE

Blackbean

parenchyma tissue. Grain is generally straight but may be interlocked, producing a decorative effect. The wood is coarse-textured.

Properties
Weighs about 44 lb/ft^3. Is difficult to dry and slow air drying is needed before kilning to avoid splitting. Tends to degrade and doesn't respond well to reconditioning. There's medium movement in service. It has medium strength in most categories but doesn't withstand shock. It has poor steam-bending properties.

Workability
Difficult to machine, soft patches of lighter tissue crumble during

planing or molding unless cutters are kept sharp. Moderate blunting effect. Screws and nails satisfactorily, but gives variable gluing results.

Preservation
Sapwood is permeable and liable to attack by the powder post beetle. Heartwood is very resistant to preservation treatment.

Uses
High-class furniture, cabinet-making and interior joinery. Good for turnery, sculpture, carving, heavy construction work, and veneers. Check with your local environmental group or supplier before buying.

CEDRUS SPP. *FAMILY:* PINACEAE

Cedar

Where it grows
The *Cedrus* species are the true cedars, growing variously in Algeria and Morocco, the western Himalayas, India, and Lebanon.

Appearance
Heartwood is light brown with a prominent growth ring, quite distinct from the lighter sapwood. Deodar cedar is straight-grained, but Atlantic and Lebanon cedars are usually knotty, with much grain disturbance.

Properties
Weight averages about 35 lb/ft^3. Dries easily with medium movement in use. Has medium bending strength but is low in other strength properties, and has a poor steam-bending rating.

Workability
Works easily with hand and machine tools, with only slight blunting, but machine cutters should be kept sharp. Durable with good holding properties, and stains, varnishes, paints, or polishes to a good finish.

Preservation
Sapwood liable to attack by the pinhole borer and longhorn beetle; heartwood resistant to preservative treatment. Sapwood varies from moderately resistant to permeable.

Uses
Furniture, interior joinery and doors; lower grades are used for paving blocks, sleepers, bridge building and house construction. Knotty material is used for garden furniture. Selected logs are sliced for veneers. Check with your local environmental group or supplier before buying.

CEDRELA SPP. *FAMILY:* MELIACEAE

South American Cedar

Where it grows
Not a true cedar (*Cedrus* spp.). The name "cedar" has been given to many hardwoods of similar fragrance, which occur in almost every country south of the USA, with the exception of Chile.

Appearance
The pale pink-brown young trees aren't so straight-grained, but have a fine texture. Darker types are from mature, slow-grown trees and are more resinous and straight-grained, but often interlocked and with a coarser texture.

Properties
Weight varies from 23-47 lb/ft^3 (average: 30 lb/ft^3). It is very stable in use. Has medium density and strength in all categories, and a moderately good steam-bending rating.

Workability
Easy to work with hand or machine tools, with low resistance to cutters, which should be kept sharp to avoid woolliness.

Preservation
The wood is durable, but the sapwood is liable to attack by the powder post beetle. The heartwood is extremely resistant to preservation treatment, but the sapwood is permeable.

Uses
High-quality cabinets, furniture, chests, interior joinery, paneling, boat-building; and is rotary-cut for plywood and sliced for veneers. Check with your local environmental group or supplier before buying.

CERATOPETALUM APETALEM *FAMILY:* CUNONACEAE

Coachwood

straight grain with fine rays, producing a flecked figure on quarter-sawn surfaces. Has a fine, even texture.

Properties
Weighs about 39 lb/ft^3. Dries fairly rapidly with a tendency to split and warp. Has medium movement in use and is of medium density, bending strength, stiffness and shock resistance, but with a high crushing strength and a good steam-bending classification.

Workability
Works easily with hand and machine tools and gives a smooth finish, although may chip out at tool exits when drilling or mortising, and nailing needs pre-boring. Glues easily and takes stain well.

Preservation
Sapwood liable to attack by the powder post beetle. The wood is non-durable, but permeable for preservation treatment.

Uses
Furniture, cabinet-making, wall paneling. Used extensively in Australia for interior joinery and moldings, and favored for bent work. Also good for gunstocks and parts of musical instruments, and appears in light domestic flooring.

Where it grows
This medium-sized Australian tree grows in New South Wales and Queensland. It is also known as scented satinwood.

Appearance
Light brown to pink-brown sapwood, not clearly demarcated from the only slightly darker-colored heartwood. Has a close,

---

CERCIDIPHYLLUM JAPONICUM *FAMILY:* TROCHODENDRACEAE

Katsura

Appearance
The heartwood is a light medium nut-brown. Logs taken for lumber are straight-grained with a very fine, compact and even texture and high luster. The plain appearance of the background color is relieved by the light narrow lines of the growth rings.

Properties
Soft and compact (29 lb/ft^3). Dries easily without distortion or degrade, and is stable in use. Of low density and medium bending and crushing strengths, with low stiffness and resistance to shock. It has a moderately good steam-bending rating.

Workability
A delight to work with using hand and machine tools, and provides a smooth surface. Doesn't hold nails or fastenings well, but glues, takes stain and polishes with ease.

Preservation
The sapwood is liable to insect attack. The wood is non-durable but permeable for preservation treatment.

Uses
Sculpture, carving, pattern-making in foundries, moldings, engravings, cabinet-making, high-class interior joinery. Check with your local environmental group or supplier before buying.

Where it grows
This valuable tree grows mainly in the northern temperate forests of Japan, but also in China and Korea.

3

4

5
5
4
6
S

CHAMAECYPARIS LAWSONIANA *FAMILY:* CUPRESSACEAE

Port Orford Cedar

Where it grows
This is being planted in a range of other countries, but grows over a limited range, scattered along the edge of the coastal forests of south-western Oregon and north-west California. Other names are Lawson's cypress (UK) and Oregon cedar (USA).

Appearance
The heartwood is a pale pink-brown, and not clearly defined from the sapwood. Has straight grain and a fine, even texture. Sometimes there's an orange-yellow resin exudation.

Properties
Weighs about 30 lb/ft^3, dries readily with little degrade, and is stable in use. Has medium bending and crushing strength, low stiffness, but good resistance to shock, with a very poor steam-bending classification.

Workability
Good with hand and machine tools, and has only a slight blunting effect. Holds screws and nails without difficulty. Can be glued satisfactorily, gives good results with stain, etc.

Preservation
Damage by longhorn beetle is often present, and sometimes by

Sirex. The wood is moderately durable, but the sapwood is permeable with oil-based preservatives by pressure or boron salts by the diffusion process.

Uses
Building boats and ships, oars, canoe paddles, arrows; also interior joinery and furniture, plus veneers.

3
4
5
5
6
6
S

CHAMAECYPARIS NOOTKATENSIS *FAMILY:* CUPRESSACEAE

Yellow Cedar

Where it grows
Although it is native to the narrow coastal belt from Alaska down to northern Oregon, the largest sizes grow in Alaska and north British Columbia. It is also known as Alaska yellow cedar and nootka false cypress in the USA, and yellow cypress and Pacific Coast yellow cedar in Canada.

Appearance
Pale yellow and straight-grained with a fine, even texture.

Properties
Weight is about 31 lb/ft^3. The wood should dry slowly to avoid surface checking in thick stock.

Noted for durability and stability once dried, the lumber is moderately strong, with medium bending and crushing strengths, low stiffness and resistance to shock, but a very poor steam-bending rating.

Workability
Good with hand and machine tools, with only a slight dulling on cutting edges. Holds screws and nails without difficulty, glues, takes stain, paint, and varnish satisfactorily, produces an excellent finish.

Preservation
A durable wood, resistant to preservative treatment.

Uses
Valued for high-class joinery, window frames, and finishing in houses; also for cabinet work. The Alaskan wood is heavier and is used for boats and ships, exterior joinery, cladding and shingles.

CHLOROPHORA EXCELSA *FAMILY:* MORACEAE

Iroko

Where it grows
This species grows in the moist semideciduous forests of tropical Africa, from Sierra Leone in the west to Tanzania in the east. Known as mvule (East Africa), odum (Ghana and Ivory Coast), kambala (Zaire), tule or intule (Mozambique), and moreira (Angola).

Appearance
The pale sapwood is clearly defined from the yellow-brown heartwood, which matures to a deeper brown. Grain is typically interlocked and sometimes irregular.

Properties
Weighs about 40 lb/ft^3, dries well and quickly with some degrade. Very durable, of medium density, stable in use, has medium bending and crushing strengths, very low stiffness and shock resistance, and a moderate bending rate.

Workability
Calcium carbonate deposits known as "stone" can damage cutting edges, and tipped or hardened saw teeth are required. Nailing, screwing, and gluing are satisfactory.

Preservation
Sapwood is liable to attack by the powder post beetle. Wood is very durable and resistant to preservation treatment, but the sapwood is classed as permeable.

Uses
High-class interior and exterior joinery, counter and laboratory bench tops, draining boards, sculpture and carving, and turnery. Widely used for ships and boats, and park benches. Check with your local environmental group or supplier before buying.

CORDIA SPP. *FAMILY:* BORAGINACEAE

African Cordia

Where it grows
The African species is deciduous and occurs in the semitropical rainforests of Kenya, Tanzania and also Nigeria. Others of the species occur in Kenya, Uganda, and Nigeria.

Appearance
The cream-colored sapwood is distinct from the heartwood, which varies from golden to medium brown. It usually darkens on maturity. Grain varies from fairly straight to interlocked or irregular, and the rays give an attractive figure.

Properties
Weighs about 27 lb/ft^3, and dries well without too much splitting or warping. Is stable in service, has low density, low bending strength, very low stiffness, medium crushing strength, very low shock resistance, and a poor steam-bending rating.

Workability
Works easily with hand and machine tools, but cutters should be kept very sharp to prevent a woolly surface. Nailing and gluing are satisfactory.

Preservation
Outer heartwood is very durable, but inner heartwood is only moderately durable and resistant to preservative treatment.

Uses
Decorative parts of furniture when strength is unimportant; also used locally for drums and sound boards because of its resonant properties. Is traditional for canoes and boats in West Africa. Check with your local environmental group or supplier before buying.

The side icons for Iroko read: 2, 2, 6, 8, 6, 6, H

The side icons for African Cordia read: 2, 2, 4, 7, 4, 5, H

CUPRESSUS SPP. *FAMILY:* CUPRESSACEAE

East African Cypress

Where it grows
Indigenous conifers in Africa are restricted mostly to the Mediterranean region or the high montane forests of central and eastern Africa, and have been introduced into South Africa.

Appearance
Heartwood is yellow to pinkish-brown, sapwood paler and up to 4 in. wide. The wood is straight-grained and the texture fine and fairly even.

Properties
It weighs about 28 lb/ft^3, is strong in relation to its weight, but has poor steam-bending properties because of knots. It dries fairly easily with little degrade, and is stable in service.

Workability
Works well with both hand and machine tools with little dulling of cutters, although knots may be troublesome. Take care when working endgrain to prevent breakout at tool exits. The wood screws, nails, and glues well, and accepts all finishing treatments.

Preservation
Is highly resistant to both insect and fungal attack and is resistant to preservation treatment.

Uses
External constructional work where the wood is in contact with the ground; also in exterior joinery, boat- and shipbuilding, and the manufacture of farmhouse-style furniture, closet linings etc. Check with your local environmental group before buying.

DALBERGIA SPP. *FAMILY:* LEGUMINOSAE

Rosewood, Brazilian & Honduras

Where it grows
Brazilian rosewood has been a treasured wood for centuries, but some are becoming very rare. It is also known as Bahia rosewood or Rio rosewood in the USA and UK, and as jacaranda in Brazil.

Appearance
Heartwood is a rich brown with variegated streaks of golden-to-chocolate and from violet to purple-black – sharply demarcated from the more creamy sapwood. Grain is mostly straight to wavy, the texture coarse, oily and gritty to the touch. Honduras rosewood has pinkish to purple-brown heartwood with irregular black markings, is straight-grained with a medium-to-fine texture.

Properties
Brazilian weighs 53 lb/ft^3, and Honduras around 58-68 lb/ft^3. Both air-dry fairly slowly, with a marked tendency to check, but are stable in service, with high strength in all categories but are low in stiffness, and have good steam-bending capabilities.

Workability
Fairly easy to work, but with severe blunting effect. Both very durable.

Preservation
Both are extremely resistant to preservative treatment.

Uses
High-class furniture, superior cabinet-making, paneling, and furniture; also piano cases and billiard and pool tables; excellent for turnery. Check with your local environmental group or supplier before buying.

Where it grows

Occurs mainly in Brazil, where it is also known as violete; known as violetta, violet wood (USA), and bois violet (France).

Appearance

The heartwood is a rich violet-brown background color shading

DALBERGIA CEARENSIS *FAMILY:* LEGUMINOSAE

DALBERGIA CEARENSIS *FAMILY:* LEGUMINOSAE

Kingwood

to black with variegated stripes or streaks of black, violet-black or violet-brown, and sometimes golden yellow. The almost white sapwood is clearly defined. The heartwood has a bright luster, a fine uniform texture and a very smooth surface.

Properties

Very heavy (75 lb/ft^3). Care is needed in air-drying to avoid splits, but it kiln-dries without degrade and is stable in use. Very strong in all categories.

Workability

Works fairly well with both hand and machine tools, if cutters are

kept very sharp. Moderate blunting effect on tools. Good nail and screwing properties, but needs pre-boring.

Preservation

This wood is durable and extremely resistant to preservative treatment.

Uses

Is in great demand for restoration and reproduction furniture, and for decorative work generally. Excellent for turnery, small fancy items, and sculpture; is in demand in veneer form for inlays and marquetry. Check with your local environmental group or supplier before buying.

Where it grows

A large tree that grows best in southern India. It is also known as East Indian rosewood and Bombay rosewood, and in India has various names, including shisham, sissoo, and biti.

Appearance

The sapwood is pale yellow-cream with a purplish tinge, and is clearly defined from the medium-to-dark,

DALBERGIA LATIFOLIA *FAMILY:* LEGUMINOSAE

Indian Rosewood

purple brown heartwood. Produces an attractive ribbon-striped grain figure on quartered surfaces, with a uniform and moderately coarse texture.

Properties

Weighs about 53 lb/ft^3, and slower drying improves the color. It is stable in use, very dense, with high bending and crushing strengths, medium resistance to shock, low stiffness, and a good steam-bending rating.

Workability

Fairly difficult to machine or work with hand tools, causing severe blunting; is unsuitable for nailing or screwing, but glues satisfactorily.

Preservation

The sapwood is liable to attack by the powder post beetle but the heartwood is very durable and resistant to preservative treatment.

Uses

Top-class furniture and cabinet work, store, office, and bank fitting. Good for turnery and is used for parts of musical instruments, exterior joinery, and decorative flooring. Check with your local environmental group before buying.

DALBERGIA MELANOXYLON *FAMILY:* LEGUMINOSAE

African Blackwood

Where it grows

A multi-stemmed, small tree that occurs in East Africa – chiefly Mozambique, where it's called Mozambique ebony, and Tanzania, where it's known as mpingo. It is not an ebony, and is closely related to the rosewoods.

Appearance

Narrow white sapwood is defined from the heartwood, which is dark purplish-brown with black streaks, giving it a black appearance. Has straight to irregular grain with a very fine texture.

Properties

Very hard and dense, weighing 75 lb/ft³. Needs to dry extremely slowly and seasoned carefully to avoid checking. Very stable in service and holds its dimensions well. Very durable and strong in all categories, and straight-grained stock has good steam-bending properties.

Workability

Stellite or tungsten-carbide-tipped saws are advised to minimize severe blunting. Pre-bore for nailing and screwing. Glues satisfactorily and polishes to a smooth finish.

Preservation

Sapwood is liable to attack by the powder post beetle; heartwood is very durable and extremely resistant to preservative treatment.

Uses

Widely used in musical instruments; also for ornamental and plain turnery. In Africa it is extensively used for carving, and for inlay work. Check with your local environmental group or supplier before buying.

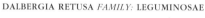

DALBERGIA RETUSA *FAMILY:* LEGUMINOSAE

Cocobolo

Where it grows

Also known as granadillo, it occurs along the Pacific seaboard of Central America from Mexico to Panama.

Appearance

When freshly cut, the heartwood is an array of colors from lemon-orange to deep rich red with variegated streaks. Grain varies from straight to irregular and is sometimes wavy, with a fine, medium, uniform texture.

Properties

Weight varies from 61-75 lb/ft³ (average 68 lb/ft³). Dries out slowly, with a tendency to check and split, but is very stable in service. Has high mechanical strength in all categories, but this is not important because of the end use.

Workability

Not unduly difficult to work with hand and machine tools, but there's moderate blunting of edges, which should be kept very sharp. Difficult to glue owing to high natural oiliness.

Preservation

The heartwood is very durable and resistant to preservative treatment.

Uses

Ideal for turnery, and used for cutlery handles, knife and tool handles, truncheons, and bowling bowls. Also highly valued for sculpture and carving; and selected logs are sliced for veneers, inlays, and paneling. Check with your local environmental group before buying.

DOISPYRUS SPP. *FAMILY:* EBENACEAE

African Ebony

species have a very attractive black and dark brown striped heartwood, usually straight-grained to slightly interlocked or curly, and the texture is very fine and even.

Properties
Weighs about 64 lb/ft^3. Air-dries fairly rapidly but is liable to surface checking, although kiln-drying causes little degrade. Very stable in service, dense, has very high strength properties and a good bending rating.

Workability
Difficult to work with either hand or machine tools as there is severe blunting. Needs a reduced cutting angle when planing the curly grain of quartered stock; needs pre-boring for screwing and nailing.

Preservation
The heartwood is very durable and extremely resistant to preservative treatment.

Uses
Sculpture, carving; excellent for turnery and handles, as well as in musical instruments and luxury cabinet work, marquetry and inlays. Check with your local environmental group or supplier before buying.

Where it grows
Mostly in southern Nigeria, Ghana, Cameroons and Zaire, and takes the name of its country or port of origin, e.g. Cameroon ebony, etc.

Appearance
The black heartwood of ebony has been in great demand since ancient Egyptian times. *D. crassiflora* is thought to be blackest, while other

---

DOISPYRUS SPP. *FAMILY:* EBENACEAE

East Indian Ebony

jet-black. Macassar ebony is medium brown with beige and black stripes. Coromandel and calamander ebony refer to heartwood with gray or brown mottled figure. Grain varies from straight to wavy, with a fine, even texture and a metallic luster.

Properties
Ceylon weighs about 73 lb/ft^3; others between 64-68 lb/ft^3; Indian is much lighter (55 lb/ft^3). Ebony develops cracks and checks if not dried slowly, has strength in all categories but can be brittle. Sapwood has a good steam-bending rating.

Workability
Heartwood is very difficult to machine with severe blunting, and increased pressure should be applied to prevent the wood rising or chattering on the cutters.

Preservation
Subject to beetle attack but is very durable and extremely resistant to preservative treatment.

Uses
Luxury furniture, sculpture, carving, turnery, handles, musical instrument parts, and inlays. Check with your local environmental group before buying.

Where it grows
Ceylon ebony (*D. ebenum*) is known as true ebony as its heartwood has a uniform jet-black color. It occurs in Sri Lanka and southern India, where it is known as tendu, tuki, or ebans.

Appearance
The sapwood is a light gray, but the heartwood of Ceylon ebony is

Sidebar (African Ebony): 8, 8, 10, 10, 10, 10, 10, H

Sidebar (East Indian Ebony): 9, 8, 10, 10, 10, 10, 10, H

DOISPYRUS VIRGINIANA *FAMILY:* EBENACEAE

Persimmon

Where it grows
A member of the ebony family, this is known as white ebony, and occurs in the central and southern states of the USA, where it is known as bara bara, boa wood, butter wood, possum wood, and Virginia date palm.

Appearance
Has a small heartwood core with variegated brown to black streaks. The valuable sapwood is off-white with a gray tint and straight-grained with a fine even texture.

Properties
Weighs 52 lb/ft^3, and gives large movement in service with changes in humidity. Very dense, has high bending and crushing strengths, and medium stiffness and shock resistance. Suitable for steam-bending to a moderate radius.

Workability
A very tough wood which works readily with machine and hand tools, but has a moderate blunting effect, so keep edges sharp. Requires pre-boring for screwing or nailing, can be glued without problems and polished to an exceptionally smooth, lustrous finish.

Preservation
Sapwood is liable to attack by the powder post beetle; the heartwood is durable and is resistant to preservative treatment.

Uses
The sapwood is used for textile shuttles, golf-club heads, and as turnery wood for striking-tool handles.

DIPTEROCARPUS SPP. *FAMILY:* DIPTEROCARPACEAE

Keruing

Where it grows
These evergreen hardwood trees grow throughout south-east Asia – in India, Burma, Thailand, Malaysia, Indonesia, and the Philippines.

Appearance
The heartwood varies in color from pink-brown to dark brown, and is rather plain in appearance. The grain is usually straight to shallowly interlocked with a moderately coarse but even texture.

Properties
Weighs 45-50 lb/ft^3, is difficult to air-dry without degrade. There's medium to large movement in service. These woods have high bending and crushing strength, high stiffness and medium shock resistance. Keruing from Sabah has a moderate bending rating.

Workability
Some samples exude resin, which causes difficulty in machining, so tungsten-carbide-tipped tools are best. Despite moderate to severe blunting, straight-grained lumber can be machined with a fibrous finish. The resin content needs care in gluing and finishing, and also penetrates most paints and varnishes.

Preservation
The sapwood is liable to attack by the powder post beetle; the heartwood is moderately durable and is resistant, often extremely so, to preservative treatment.

Uses
Construction, frames, sides, flooring for vehicles and buildings, some exterior construction; also rotary cut for plywood and sliced for veneers. Check with your local environmental group or supplier before buying.

DISTEMONANTHUS BENTHAMIANUS *FAMILY:* LEGUMINOSAE

Ayan

a fine and even texture and lustrous surface.

Where it grows

This tree occurs throughout tropical West Africa from Ivory Coast to Gabon and Zaire.

Appearance

The sapwood is pale yellow and not clearly demarcated from the heartwood, which varies in color from yellow to golden brown. Grain is often irregular and interlocked, sometimes wavy, with

Properties

Weight varies from 37-48 lb/ft^3, averaging around 42 lb/ft^3. Has very good dimensional stability, is dense, has medium bending strength and high crushing strength, with low stiffness and shock resistance and good compression strength along the grain. Has a moderate bending classification.

Workability

Fairly difficult to machine, with moderate to severe blunting caused by silica in the wood. Gum build-up on saws requires an increased set. Nailing needs pre-boring.

Preservation

Moderately durable, showing some resistance to termites in West Africa. The heartwood is resistant to preservative treatment.

Uses

Exterior joinery, doors, window frames and sills, and ships' fittings; also for interior joinery, furniture, cabinet work, and road and railroad vehicle building. Makes ideal gym floors. Logs are rotary cut for plywood and sliced for decorative veneers. Check with your local environmental group before buying.

ENDIANDRA PALMERSTONII *FAMILY:* LAURACEAE

Queensland Walnut

Where it grows

This Australian tree is not a true walnut (*Juglans* spp.). It grows abundantly in northern Queensland.

Appearance

Bears a striking resemblance to European walnut, but has a more prominent striped figure. The pinkish sapwood is narrow, and the heartwood varies from gray to pale mid-brown, and often to dark brown, with pinkish, gray-green or purple-black streaks. Grain is interlocked and often wavy.

Properties

Weighs about 42 lb/ft^3, tends to air-dry fairly rapidly with some tendency to split at the ends; kiln-dries rapidly in thinner sizes without checking, but tends to warp. There's medium movement in service. It has medium bending strength and shock resistance, low stiffness, and high crushing strength, with a moderate steam-bending classification.

Workability

Difficult to work, requiring carbide-tipped saws and high-speed cutters to overcome blunting. Gluing is satisfactory and holding properties are good.

Preservation

The heartwood is non-durable and resistant to preservative treatment but the sapwood is permeable.

Uses

Store, office, and bank fitting, high-class cabinets and furniture, interior joinery and many forms of decorative work; flooring; logs are rotary cut for plywood; or sliced for veneer.

4
▲
2
✿
6
⚒
8
∿
4
▣
6
H

ENTANDROPHRAGMA ANGOLENSE *FAMILY:* MELIACEAE

Gedu Nohor

Where it grows
This large deciduous tree grows in the semi-evergreen forests of West, central and East Africa, from Uganda in the east to Angola and Ivory Coast in the West.

Appearance
The heartwood has a rather dull, plain appearance of light reddish-brown with a fairly interlocked grain. Some logs are much lighter, pale pinkish-gray, similar to the pinkish-gray sapwood.

Properties
Weighs about 34 lb/ft^3, and is stable in service, drying quite rapidly with some distortion. Has medium density and crushing strength, low bending strength and shock resistance, and very low stiffness, with a poor steam-bending classification.

Workability
Works fairly easily with hand and machine tools, but the interlocked grain has a moderate blunting effect. Nailing is satisfactory.

Preservation
The sapwood is liable to attack by the powder post beetle; heartwood is moderately durable but extremely resistant to preservative treatment.

Uses
Often used as a substitute for mahogany in furniture and cabinet-making for interior parts, partitions, edge lippings, and facings; also for interior and exterior joinery, store and office fitting. Good for domestic flooring, and is used in boats, cabins, and planking. Check with your local environmental group or supplier before buying.

6
▲
4
✿
6
⚒
8
∿
6
▣
8
H

ENTANDROPHRAGMA CYLINDRICUM *FAMILY:* MELIACEAE

Sapele

Where it grows
This grows widely in the tropical rainforests of West, central, and East Africa, from Ivory Coast through Ghana and Nigeria to the Cameroons, and eastwards to Uganda, Zaire, and Tanzania.

Appearance
The narrow sapwood is pale yellow-white and the heartwood salmon pink when freshly cut, maturing into reddish-brown. It has a closely interlocked grain, resulting in a pencil-striped or roe figure on quartered surfaces. Wavy grain yields a fiddleback or mottled figure with a fine, even texture.

Properties
Weighs 35-43 lb/ft^3, averaging about 39 lb/ft^3. Dries fairly rapidly, with a tendency to distort. Has medium movement in service, medium density, bending and shock resistance, high crushing strength, low stiffness, and a poor steam-bending rating.

Workability
Good with both hand and machine tools, with moderate blunting. Nailing and gluing are satisfactory.

Preservation
Sapwood is liable to attack by the powder post beetle and moderately resistant to preservative treatment. Heartwood is durable but very resistant to preservative treatment.

Uses
High-quality furniture and cabinet-making; interior and exterior joinery; boat and vehicle building; piano cases and sports goods; ideal for decorative flooring. Check with your local environmental group or supplier before buying.

ENTANDROPHRAGMA UTILE *FAMILY:* MELIACEAE

Utile

uniform reddish-brown mahogany color with an interlocked, irregular grain.

Properties
Weight varies from 34-47 lb/ft^3 with an average of 41 lb/ft^3. Dries with some distortion, but not severe. There's medium movement in service. It is dense, with high crushing strength and medium bending strength, low stiffness and shock resistance, and a very poor steam-bending rating.

Workability
Works well with both hand and machine tools, with only moderate blunting. Takes screws and nails satisfactorily, and is easy to glue.

Preservation
Heartwood is durable but the sapwood is liable to attack by the powder post beetle. Heartwood is extremely resistant to both decay and preservatives.

Uses
Furniture and cabinets, counter tops, interior and exterior joinery, interior construction work, stores and offices, and domestic flooring, as well as boats, musical instruments, and sports goods. It is also cut for plywood and veneers. Check with your local environmental group or supplier before buying.

Where it grows
This tree grows in the moist, deciduous high forests of tropical West and East Africa, Sierra Leone, Cameroons, Liberia, Gabon, Uganda, and Angola, with commercial supplies coming from Ivory Coast and Ghana.

Appearance
The light-brown sapwood is distinct from the heartwood, which is a

---

EUCALYPTUS DELEGATENSIS *FAMILY:* MYRTACEAE

Tasmanian Oak

a narrow, indistinct, paler sapwood. Usually straight-grained, but sometimes interlocked or wavy, and with a coarse texture.

Properties
The three species range from 39 lb/ft^3 to 49 lb/ft^3 on average. The wood dries readily and fairly quickly but may develop surface checks and distort. Has medium bending strength, shock resistance, and stiffness, with high crushing strength. Only one, *E. obliqua,* has a moderate steam-bending rating.

Workability
All three work well with both hand and machine tools, and hold nails

and screws well. Can be glued easily, take stain and polish well.

Preservation
Sapwood is prone to the powder post beetle; heartwood is moderately durable and resistant to preservative treatment, but the sapwood is permeable.

Uses
Used extensively for interior and exterior joinery and building construction, cladding, and weatherboards; also used for furniture, cooperage, and agricultural implements, among other things.

Where it grows
Three species of *Eucalyptus* occur in south-eastern Australia from New South Wales to Tasmania.

Appearance
The heartwood varies from pale cookie to light brown with a pinkish tinge, and the species have

EUCALYPTUS DIVERSICOLOR *FAMILY:* MYRTACEAE

Karri

Where it grows
This is an important tree to south-western Australia, and grows to an immense 279 ft.

Appearance
The heartwood is a uniform reddish-brown with an interlocked grain, producing a striped figure on quartered surfaces. Texture is moderately coarse, but even.

Properties
Average weight is 55 lb/ft³. Needs great care in drying and is prone to deep checking in thick stock, and distortion in thin. There's large movement in service, but this heavy lumber is high in all strength categories and has a moderate steam-bending classification (except when small knots are present).

Workability
Difficult to work with hand tools and fairly hard to machine, because the grain has a moderate to severe blunting effect. Pre-boring is needed for nailing and screwing, but it glues well and can be brought to an excellent finish.

Preservation
Heartwood is durable and very resistant to preservative, but the sapwood is classified as permeable.

Uses
Used above water for wharf and bridge construction and in shipbuilding; also for joists and heavy beams; while selected pieces are used in furniture, cabinet fittings, and domestic flooring, as well as for plywood and veneers.

EUCALYPTUS MARGINATA *FAMILY:* MYRTACEAE

Jarrah

Where it grows
More jarrah is cut than any other Australian commercial timber. It's found in the coastal region south of Perth in Western Australia, and large quantities are exported.

Appearance
Heartwood is a rich dark reddish-brown, with occasional gum veins and pockets that detract from its appearance, but with boat-shaped flecks that enhance it. Grain is usually fairly straight, sometimes wavy and interlocked, with a moderately coarse but even texture.

Properties
Weight varies between 43-65 lb/ft³, averaging 51 lb/ft³. Will distort unless air-dried before kilning. There's medium shrinkage in service; it has medium bending strength and stiffness, high crushing strength, and a moderate steam-bending rating.

Workability
It's fairly hard to machine and not good for hand tools because of its hardness and density. There is moderate blunting effect. Pre-boring is necessary for nailing and screwing, but it glues and finishes well.

Preservation
Heartwood is durable and resistant to insect attack and preservative treatment but sapwood is classified as permeable.

Uses
Ideal for construction such as dock pilings, harbor work, and other marine uses; makes good railroad sleepers, flooring, shingles, weatherboards, rafters; turnery, plywood, and veneers.

Where it grows

This one is often confused with Sri Lanka satinwood, and grows in Bermuda, the Bahamas, and southern Florida, but reaches its best development in Jamaica.

Appearance

The heartwood is rich cream to golden yellow, with a straight to interlocked, wavy or irregular grain;

FAGARA FLAVA *FAMILY:* RUTACEAE

West Indian Satinwood

the texture is fine and even with a bright, satin luster.

Properties

Very heavy and dense (about 56 lb/ft^3), and requires care in drying to avoid distortion. Has low impact strength, moderate stiffness, and a low bending strength.

Workability

Works well with hand and machine tools, but there is high resistance to cutting, and edges should be kept very sharp where irregular grain is present, and a reduced cutting angle is recommended. The fine dust caused by machining can

cause dermatitis. The wood requires pre-boring for nailing or screwing, but glues and takes polish well.

Preservation

The wood is non-durable and extremely resistant to impregnation.

Uses

Exported in only small quantities and is used for furniture, high-class cabinet-making, reproduction and restoration; excellent for turnery; also used for veneers. Check with your local environmental group before buying.

Where it grows

Beech grows in the northern temperate regions of America, Canada, and Europe, western Asia, Japan, and northern Africa.

Appearance

Very pale cream to pinkish-brown, and often "weathered" to a deep

FAGUS SPP. *FAMILY:* FAGACEAE

Beech

reddish-bronze-brown after steaming. Is typically straight-grained with broad rays and a fine, even texture.

Properties

Japanese beech is the lightest (39 lb/ft^3) and American is the heaviest (46 lb/ft^3). Dries rapidly but shrinks in service. It has medium strength in bending, stiffness, and shock resistance, and high crushing strength, with a very good steam-bending rating.

Workability

Works well with hand and machine tools and has good holding properties; it glues very easily and finishes excellently.

Preservation

Prone to the common furniture beetle and death watch beetle. The sapwood is affected by the longhorn beetle. Beech is classified as permeable for preservative treatment.

Uses

It's the most popular wood for furniture, desks and the like, and interior joinery; and, when treated, for exterior joinery. Also used for turnery, domestic woodware, sports goods, parts of musical instruments, plywood and unremarkable decorative veneers.

FLINDERSIA SPP. *FAMILY:* RUTACEAE

Queensland Maple

Where it grows
As its name suggests, it grows in northern Queensland, and also occurs in Papua New Guinea (but it is not a true maple). There are a few closely related species: *F. brayleyana*, *F. pimenteliana*, and *F. laevicarpa*.

Appearance
The heartwood is pale brown to pink with a silken luster, and matures to pale brown. Grain is often interlocked, sometimes wavy or curly.

Properties
The weights range from 34-43 lb/ft^3. They air- and kiln-dry satisfactorily but with tendency to collapse; distortion may need kiln reconditioning. There's medium shrinkage in service. Wood has medium bending and crushing strengths, low stiffness and resistance to shock, and a poor steam-bending rating.

Workability
Works well with hand and machine tools with moderate blunting. Interlocked grain will pick up on quartered stock, so a reduced angle is necessary. Holds screws well, glues satisfactorily.

Preservation
The heartwood is moderately durable and resistant to preservative treatment, and is not subject to insect attack.

Uses
High-class cabinets and furniture, interior fittings and moldings, interior joinery; specialist uses such as vehicle body work, gunstocks, printing blocks; is cut for plywood and veneers. Check with your local environmental group or supplier before buying.

FLINDERSIA SCHOTTIANA *FAMILY:* RUTACEAE

Southern Silver Ash

Where it grows
There are many *Flindersia* species growing in Australia producing lumber with names such as ash and maple, but are botanically unrelated.

Appearance
The pale cookie-colored heartwood is mostly straight-grained, but sometimes shallowly interlocked or wavy, with a medium texture.

Properties
Weight varies but an average is 35 lb/ft^3. It dries rather slowly and is prone to warp slightly, but can be kiln-dried up to about 2 in. thick with little degrade. Is stable in service, with medium bending and crushing strength, low stiffness and resistance to shock, and a good steam-bending classification.

Workability
Good with hand and machine tools, with only moderate blunting. Quartered surfaces tend to pick up interlocked grain when planing or molding. Has good nail- and screw-holding properties.

Preservation
The heartwood is very durable above ground and resistant to preservative treatment, but the sapwood is classified as permeable.

Uses
High-class cabinets and furniture, interior trim and fitments, interior and exterior joinery; is used in food containers as it is odorless and will not taint. A good structural timber, is popular for turnery and produces plywood and veneers. Check with your local environmental group before buying.

Where it grows

Ash thrives throughout Europe, North America, and Japan. *F. americana* is known as white ash (Canada); *F. pennsylvania*, American ash, is known as green ash (USA) or red ash (Canada).

Appearance

American is gray-brown with a reddish tinge, while European is

FRAXINUS SPP. *FAMILY:* OLEACEAE

Ash

creamy-white to light brown, sometimes with a dark brown to black heart. It is straight-grained and coarse-textured with a decorative figure.

Properties

Weight varies from 36-43 lb/ft^3. Dries fairly rapidly with little degrade and minimal shrinkage, has medium bending and crushing strength and shock resistance, low stiffness, and an excellent steam-bending rating.

Workability

Works with hand and machine tools; pre-boring needed for

nailing. Glues easily; takes stains and polishes well.

Preservation

The heartwood is moderately resistant to preservative treatment, but the black heartwood is resistant.

Uses

Used extensively for chairs and in cabinet-making, furniture and interior joinery; specialist uses include tool handles, bent handles for umbrellas, store fitting, vehicles, wheelwrighting, and agricultural implements. Also used for boats, canoes, sports goods, turnery; is sliced for veneers.

Where it grows

The tree grows in freshwater swamps on the west coasts of Sarawak and throughout Malaysia and south-east Asia. *G. macrophyllum* and *G. bancanus* produce melawis in western Malaysia.

Appearance

The sapwood is up to 2 in. wide but is not clearly defined from the

GONYSTYLUS MACROPHYLLUM *FAMILY:* GONYSTYLACEAE

Ramin

heartwood, which is a uniform creamy-white to pale straw color with a featureless straight to shallowly interlocked grain and a moderately fine and even texture.

Properties

Ramin weighs 40-45 lb/ft^3, averaging about 41 lb/ft^3. Melawis weighs about 44 lb/ft^3. Air-dry stock is easily kilned without degrade but may stain and needs dipping after conversion. There's large movement in service. This dense wood has a high bending and crushing strength, low shock resistance, and medium stiffness, with a very poor steam-bending rating.

Workability

Works fairly easily by hand and machine, with moderate blunting, but the grain tends to tear on quartered material. Pre-bore for nailing.

Preservation

The heartwood is perishable; the sapwood liable to attack by the powder post beetle, but is permeable for preservation treatment.

Uses

Furniture, fittings, picture frames and other moldings; carving and turnery; interior joinery; plywood and veneers. Check with your local environmental group before buying.

4

2

6

5

4

6

H

GOSSWEILERODENDRON BALSAMIFERUM *FAMILY:* LEGUMINOSAE

Agba

Where it grows
One of the largest trees in tropical West Africa, it occurs mainly in western Nigeria and also in Angola and Zaire.

Appearance
The heartwood has a uniform pale straw to tan brown color, with a straight to shallow interlocked or wavy grain, and a fine texture.

Properties
Weights about 32 lb/ft^3. Drying is fairly rapid with little degrade, but with exudation of dark oleo-resin. There's small movement in service, and the wood has a moderately

good steam-bending rating, with very low stiffness and low bending strength and shock resistance, and a medium crushing strength. Nailing is satisfactory.

Preservation
Very resistant to decay but the sapwood is liable to attack by the common furniture beetle. The heartwood is resistant to preservative treatment, but the sapwood is permeable.

Uses
Excellent for interior joinery; is used as a substitute for oak for school desks and church furniture, and for

moldings; also good for turnery; but not so good for food items because of its resinous odor. Also used for flooring, exterior joinery, coachwork, and is cut for plywood and veneers. Check with your local environmental group or supplier before buying.

6

6

10

8

6

8

H

GOSSYPIOSPERMUM PRAECOX *FAMILY:* FLACOURTIACEAE

Maracaibo Boxwood

Where it grows
The name "boxwood" originally applied to *Buxus sempervirens* from Europe and eastern Asia, but today covers a wide range of unrelated species, occurring in Cuba and the Dominican Republic, with commercial supplies coming from Colombia and Venezuela.

Appearance
It's cream-white to lemon-yellow, with little difference between heartwood and sapwood, and has a high luster, straight grain with a fine and uniform texture.

Properties
Weighs about 50-56 lb/ft^3. Dries very slowly, with a tendency to split

and surface-check. Very stable in use, is not used for its strength, but has good steam-bending properties where discoloration is unimportant.

Workability
Works satisfactorily with hand and machine tools, but there's high resistance in cutting. Glues well, can be brought to a good, smooth finish.

Preservation
The sapwood is liable to fungal attack and is susceptible to the common furniture beetle, but the hardwood is durable. The sapwood is permeable for preservative treatment.

Uses
Outstanding for its very fine texture and excellent turning properties; used for handles, skittles and the like, textile rollers, shuttles, spindles; precision rules, drawing and measuring instruments, and engravers' blocks. Is sliced for veneers and other decorative work. Check with your local environmental group or supplier before buying.

Where it grows

Produced from three species, and is known as ironwood in the USA. They occur from southern Florida and the Bahamas through Jamaica, Cuba and the West Indies, and from Mexico down through Central America to Colombia and Venezuela.

GUAIACUM SPP. *FAMILY:* ZYGOPHYLLACEAE

Lignum Vitae

Appearance

Dark greenish-brown or nearly black, with a closely interlocked grain and a fine, even texture.

Properties

It weighs on average 77 lb/ft^3, dries slowly, is refractory and liable to check. There's medium movement in use. The wood has outstanding strength in all categories, and a very high crushing strength.

Workability

Unsuitable for bending, it is very difficult to machine and has high resistance to cutting. Gluing can be difficult, but it polishes well.

Preservation

It is extremely durable and resistant to preservation treatment.

Uses

Ideal for marine equipment because of its self-lubricating properties; is used wherever lubrication is impractical such as in wheels, guides, rollers, and blocks; in the textile industry for cotton gins; also used in die cutting. Has long been a favorite for sculpture and carving, is excellent for turnery and bowling bowls, or "woods." Check with your local environmental group before buying.

10	
10	
10	
10	
10	
10	
10	
10	
H	

Where it grows

Guarea occurs in tropical West Africa, principally Ivory Coast and Nigeria. *G. cedrata* produced white guarea, known as scented guarea in the UK, while *G. thompsonii* produces black guarea, known by various names.

GUAREA CEDRATA *FAMILY:* MELIACEAE

Guarea

Appearance

The wide sapwood is slightly paler than the heartwood, which is pale pinkish-brown with straight to interlocked grain, the straighter-grained being *G. thompsonii*. Both have a fine texture.

Properties

G. cedrata weighs 36 lb/ft^3 while *G. thompsonii* is 39 lb/ft^3. Dry fairly rapidly with little tendency to warp, and *G. thompsonii*, tending to split, needs care in drying. They're stable in use, with medium bending strength, low stiffness and resistance to shock. *G. cedrata* has medium crushing strength and a good bending rating, while

G. thompsonii has high crushing strength and a moderate bending rating.

Workability

Both species work fairly well with hand and machine tools, but may be woolly. Both glue well.

Preservation

Very durable, extremely resistant to preservative treatment, but the sapwood is permeable.

Uses

Furniture, interior fittings, edge lippings and facings; high-class joinery, boats, vehicles, floor boards; plywood and veneers. Check with your local environmental group or supplier before buying.

3	
3	
6	
5	
6	
7	
H	

GUIBOURTIA EHIE *FAMILY:* LEGUMINOSAE

Ovangkol

Where it grows
It occurs in tropical West Africa, mainly Ivory Coast, and Ghana. Supplies also come from southern Nigeria and Gabon.

Appearance
The heartwood is yellow-brown to deep chocolate-brown with grayish-black stripes. The grain is interlocked and the texture is moderately coarse.

Properties
Average weight is about 50 lb/ft^3. The wood dries rapidly and fairly well, but care is needed in kilning thick stock to avoid collapse. Medium movement in service. Has medium bending and crushing strengths and shock resistance; despite low stiffness, has a poor steam-bending rating.

Workability
Moderate resistance and blunting to cutting edges, so tools should be kept very sharp. Saws slowly but well. Good nail- and screw-holding properties, glues well.

Preservation
The heartwood is moderately durable and resistant to preservative treatment but the sapwood is permeable.

Uses
High-class furniture, cabinet-making, interior joinery, decorative work; excellent for turnery and makes hardwearing domestic flooring. Rotary cut for plywood and sliced for veneers. Check with your local environmental group before buying.

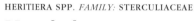

HERITIERA SPP. *FAMILY:* STERCULIACEAE

Mengkulang

Where it grows
A wide number of species of *Heritiera* occur in the tropics, including West Africa, Thailand, and the Philippines. Mengkulang is a Malay name for half a dozen or more species which occur in east Asia.

Appearance
The sapwood is pale orange, blending into the heartwood, which varies from mid-pinkish-brown to dark red-brown; grain is interlocked and sometimes irregular; texture is moderately coarse and fairly even.

Properties
Weight varies but averages 40-45 lb/ft^3, although the one known as kembang (from Sabah) is lighter. It dries rapidly and well, given to warping or surface checking in some species. Dense, stable in service, has medium bending strength, stiffness and resistance to shock, high crushing strength, and a very poor steam-bending rating.

Workability
Works moderately well but there's severe blunting of edges, especially saw teeth. Pre-bore for nailing. Glues well.

Preservation
Is perishable and the sapwood is liable to attack by the powder post beetle. Heartwood is resistant to preservative treatment, the sapwood moderately resistant.

Uses
Cabinet and furniture work, wheelwrighting, vehicle frames, paneling, sills, railroad sleepers, boat ribs, planking; also domestic flooring. Is cut and sliced for plywood and veneer. Check with your local environmental group before buying.

Courbaril

HYMENAEA COURBARIL *FAMILY:* LEGUMINOSAE

Where it grows
This almost evergreen tree grows from southern Mexico through central America and the West Indies down as far as Brazil, Bolivia, and Peru.

Appearance
The heartwood matures to an orange-red to reddish-brown, marked with russet and dark brown streaks. Often has a golden luster, and the grain is usually interlocked with a medium to coarse texture.

Properties
Dense, weighing about 56 lb/ft³. Rather difficult to dry, with surface checking and warping. Stable in service and very strong in all categories, but has low stiffness, which gives it a moderate steam-bending classification.

Workability
Moderately difficult to work, with severe blunting. Requires pre-boring for nailing, but holds screws and glues well.

Preservation
Moderately durable but non-durable when a high proportion of sapwood is present. Very resistant to termites and extremely resistant to preservative treatment.

Uses
General building, wheelwrighting, looms, carpentry and joinery; also for sports goods and striking-tool handles; ideal for ships' planking, gear cogs and so on. Sliced for highly decorative veneers suitable for cabinets and architectural paneling. Check with your local environmental group or supplier before buying.

European Holly

ILEX SPP. *FAMILY:* AQUIFOLIACEAE

Where it grows
There are about 175 different species of holly, growing in the UK and other parts of Europe from Norway, Denmark, and Germany down to the Mediterranean and west Asia.

Appearance
The heartwood is white to gray-white, sometimes with a slight greenish-gray cast, with little or no figure. The sapwood is not distinct from the heartwood. The grain tends to be irregular with a very fine, even texture.

Properties
Weighs on average about 49 lb/ft³. Fairly difficult to dry. Stable in use when dry. Heavy, dense, and tough in all strength categories, but not suitable for steam-bending.

Workability
Has high resistance to cutting and sawing and a moderate blunting effect. Turns well, requires pre-boring for screwing or nailing. Glues easily.

Preservation
In the round, logs are liable to attack by the forest longhorn or Buprestid beetle. Heartwood is perishable and sapwood liable to attack by the common furniture beetle, but is permeable for preservation treatment.

Uses
Available in limited quantities in small dimensions and narrow veneers. Mainly used as a substitute for boxwood; also dyed and used for marquetry, antique repair; also used in musical instruments.

8
10
10
8
8
10
H

8
7
8
9
8
7
H

INTSIA SPP. *FAMILY*: LEGUMINOSAE

Merbau

Where it grows
The various species grow in the Philippines, Papua New Guinea, New Britain, Malaysia, Indonesia, and Sabah.

Appearance
The sapwood is clearly defined from the white-to-pale yellow heartwood, which matures into a medium-to-dark red-brown on exposure. Grain is interlocked and sometimes wavy, with a rather coarse but even texture.

Properties
Average weight is 50 lb/ft³. It dries rapidly with little degrade, and is stable in service. It has medium bending and crushing strengths, stiffness and resistance to shock loads. Has a moderate steam-bending rating.

Workability
Moderate blunting of tools with gum tending to build up on saws. Pre-boring is necessary for nailing. Care required in gluing and the pores need considerable filling for a good finish.

Preservation
The heartwood is durable and resistant to preservative treatment.

Uses
Used locally for heavy constructional work, interior joinery, paneling, furniture, agricultural implements and striking-tool handles. Good for flooring and, when treated, is used for railroad sleepers. Selected logs are used for veneers. Check with your local environmental group before buying.

JUGLANS NIGRA *FAMILY*: JUGLANDACEAE

American Walnut/Black Walnut

Where it grows
One of the true walnut trees, widely distributed throughout North America from southern Ontario to Texas, and in the east from Maine to Florida. Is also known as black American walnut Virginia walnut (UK); walnut canaletto, black hickory nut or walnut tree (USA); and Canadian walnut (Canada and USA).

Appearance
Heartwood matures into a rich dark brown to purplish-black. Usually straight-grained, but sometimes wavy or curly. Texture is rather coarse but uniform.

Properties
Weighs about 40 lb/ft³. It requires care in drying to avoid checking and degrade. Small movement in service. Is of medium density, bending and crushing strength, with low stiffness and shock resistance; it has good steam-bending qualities.

Workability
Works well with hand and machine tools, with moderate blunting. Holds nails and screws well, and can be glued satisfactorily. A delight to work, takes stain and polish with ease and can be brought to an excellent finish.

Preservation
Sapwood liable to attack by the powder post beetle; heartwood is resistant to decay and preservative treatment, but the sapwood is permeable.

Uses
Rifle butts and gunstocks, high-class cabinets and furniture, interior joinery, musical instruments sculpture and many other uses.

JUGLANS REGIA *FAMILY:* JUGLANDACEAE

European Walnut

Where it grows
The walnut tree originated in the Himalayas, Iran, Lebanon, and Asia Minor, but today commercial supplies come from France, Italy, Turkey, and south-west Asia.

Appearance
The heartwood is usually gray-brown with irregular dark brown streaks, often forming a central core, sharply defined from the remaining plain heartwood. It has straight to wavy grain with a rather coarse texture.

Properties
Weight averages about 40 lb/ft^3. Dries well, with a tendency for checks in thicker material. There's medium shrinkage in service. It has medium bending strength and resistance to shock, with a high crushing strength and low stiffness. Has a good steam-bending rating.

Workability
Works easily and well with hand and machine tools, glues satisfactorily, and can be brought to an excellent finish.

Preservation
Heartwood is moderately durable and resistant to preservative treatment; sapwood is liable to attack by the powder post beetle, but is permeable to preservatives.

Uses
High-class cabinets, furniture, interior joinery; also popular for attractive rifle butts and gunstocks and all kinds of sports goods; a favorite for carving, turnery, and fascias for expensive cars. Produces decorative figured veneers.

JUNIPERUS SPP. *FAMILY:* CUPRESSACEAE

Pencil Cedar

Where it grows
East African pencil cedar grows in Kenya, Uganda, Tanzania, and Ethiopia; Virginian pencil cedar is found in southern Ontario and the US down to eastern Texas, and is known as Eastern red cedar in the US and pencil cedar in the UK.

Appearance
Both species mature to a uniform reddish-brown. Both are soft and straight-grained with a fine, even texture.

Properties
"East African" weighs an average 36 lb/ft^3, while "Virginia" is about 33 lb/ft^3. It needs to dry slowly to avoid checking and end splitting. Is stable in service, and has medium bending and crushing strengths, very low stiffness and shock resistance, and a poor steam-bending rating.

Workability
Straight-grained stock works readily with hand and machine tools, but knotty stock needs care in planing. It needs pre-boring for nailing, but glues well.

Preservation
The heartwood is durable and extremely resistant to preservative treatment, and the sapwood moderately resistant.

Uses
It's the standard wood for slats for lead pencils. Locally it is used for joinery, furniture and carpentry; also for linen and blanket chests because of its fragrant aroma. Check with your local environmental group or supplier before buying.

Sidebar icons (European Walnut): 6, 4, 6, 6, 6, 8, H

Sidebar icons (Pencil Cedar): 3, 3, 5, 4, 5, 6, S

KHAYA SPP. *FAMILY:* MELIACEAE

African Mahogany

Where it grows
The name African mahogany covers all trees of the *Khaya* species. The bulk of commercial lumber is from the coastal rainforests of West Africa from Ivory Coast to the Cameroons and Gabon; also from Uganda and Tanzania.

Appearance
It has a typically reddish-brown heartwood. The grain can be straight but is usually interlocked, producing a striped or roe figure on quartered surfaces.

Properties
Weight varies between 33-37 lb/ft^3 depending on species. The wood dries fairly rapidly with little degrade and is stable in use. It is of medium density and crushing strength, has a low bending strength, very low stiffness and resistance to shock loads, and a very poor steam-bending rating.

Workability
Works easily with both hand and machine tools. Nailing is satisfactory, the wood glues well and can be stained and polished to an excellent finish.

Preservation
The heartwood is moderately durable and the sapwood, liable to attack by powder post beetle, is

resistant to impregnation by preservatives.

Uses
Important for furniture, office desks, cabinet-making, handrails, paneling; also for domestic flooring, boats, and vehicles. Produces plywood and veneers. Check with your local environmental group before buying.

KNIGHTIA EXCELSA *FAMILY:* PROTEACEAE

Rewarewa

Where it grows
This crooked tree is also known as New Zealand honeysuckle.

Appearance
The heartwood is a deep red, strongly marked with dark red-brown ray figure, and is strikingly mottled on quartered surfaces. The grain is irregular and the texture is fine and lustrous.

Properties
Weighs 46 lb/ft^3. Reaction wood (formed during growing, as a "reaction" to local conditions) is often present, making it difficult to dry. It requires accurate conversion to avoid serious distortion. There is large movement in service. It has medium density and bending strength, but high stiffness, shock resistance, and crushing strength. It is not suitable for steam-bending.

Workability
Works readily with hand and machine tools, with moderately severe blunting. Nailing requires pre-boring, but it has good holding properties for screws. Glues satisfactorily. Oil finishes and varnish should be avoided.

Preservation
The heartwood is non-durable and resistant to preservative treatment, but the sapwood is permeable.

Uses
Ornamental cabinet and furniture work, interior joinery, flooring, staircases, banisters, carved fireplaces. A firm favorite for ornamental turnery. Selected logs are cut for plywood, but it is best when sliced into beautifully decorative veneers.

Where it grows
This occurs in mountainous districts from the Swiss Alps to the Carpathians of Russia. Other varieties occur in Canada, the USA, Europe, and Japan.

Appearance
The heartwood is pale reddish-brown to brick-red, with clearly

LARIX SPP. *FAMILY:* PINACEAE

Larch

marked annual rings. It has straight grain and a fine uniform texture.

Properties
Weight varies from 30-38 lb/ft^3. It dries fairly rapidly with some distortion, is stable in use, has medium bending strength, low stiffness, medium crushing strength and resistance to shock, and a moderate steam-bending rating.

Workability
Works fairly readily with both hand and machine tools. Requires pre-boring for nailing, and takes stain, paint or varnish satisfactorily.

Preservation
Moderately durable and liable to insect attack by pinhole borer, longhorn beetle, sometimes *Sirex,* and the common furniture beetle. The heartwood is resistant to preservative treatment and the sapwood is moderately resistant.

Uses
When treated, is used for mine props, stakes, transmission poles. The heartwood is good for work where durability is important: boat planking, bridge construction, railroad sleepers, exterior joinery in contact with the ground. Also cut for plywood and sliced for veneers.

5
5
7
4
7
8
S

Where it grows
It occurs from New England to Mexico and into Central America. Known in the US as gum, sweet gum, bilsted, red gum (heartwood), or sap gum (sapwood); while in the UK the names hazel pine (sapwood) and satin walnut (heartwood) can be misleading.

LIQUIDAMBAR STYRACIFLUA *FAMILY:* HAMAMELIDACEAE

American Red Gum

Appearance
The creamy-white sapwood is sold separately as sap gum, while the heartwood, sold as red gum, varies from pink-brown to a deeper reddish-brown. Grain is irregular, with a fine uniform texture and a satin-sheen luster.

Properties
Weighs about 35 lb/ft^3. The wood dries fairly rapidly, tending to warp and twist. Has medium strength in all categories and a very poor steam-bending rating.

Workability
Red gum works easily with hand and machine tools, with slight

blunting. The material takes screws and nails without difficulty and is easy to glue.

Preservation
Is non-durable and liable to insect attack. The heartwood is moderately resistant to preservative treatment, but the sapwood is permeable.

Uses
Furniture, interior trim and fittings, doors and paneling, and for interior joinery; also for dry cooperage, packing cases, crates, and pallets. Cut for plywood and sliced for veneers.

6
4
6
4
6
7
H

LIRIODENDRON TULIPIFERA *FAMILY:* MAGNOLIACEAE

American Whitewood

Where it grows
Occurs in eastern USA and Canada, where it is known as canary wood. In the UK it is called canary whitewood; also called tulip tree in the USA and UK; poplar and yellow poplar in the USA.

Appearance
The sapwood is creamy-white; the heartwood varies from yellow-brown to pale olive-brown with streaks. It is straight-grained, with a fine, even texture.

Properties
Weight is about 23-32 lb/ft^3 and the wood kiln-dries easily and well, and air-dries with little degrade.

There's little movement in service. It has medium crushing strength, low bending strength, stiffness and resistance to shock, and a medium steam-bending rating.

Workability
Works well with hand and machine, has good nailing properties, glued joints hold well, and it can be stained, painted or polished well.

Preservation
The heartwood is non-durable, and the sapwood is liable to attack by the common furniture beetle. It is moderately resistant to preservative treatment, but the sapwood is permeable.

Uses
Pattern-making, sculpture, and wood carving. Also used for interior parts of furniture, joinery, and doors, for dry cooperage, packaging, and pallets, and interior trim for boats. Extensively used for plywood and sliced for veneers.

LOPHIRA ALATA *FAMILY:* OCHNACEAE

Ekki

Where it grows
This wood grows from Sierra Leone to Nigeria and the Cameroons in the heavy rainforests and swamps.

Appearance
The pale pink sapwood is clearly demarcated from the valuable heartwood, which varies from dark purple-brown to chocolate-brown with white flecked deposits in the pores. Grain is usually interlocked, sometimes irregular, and with coarse, uneven texture.

Properties
Weighs about 59-69 lb/ft^3. Is extremely refractory and difficult to dry, and shakes badly. Serious degrade is possible in the form of

surface checking and end splitting. It exhibits large shrinkage in service, is very heavy, with very high bending strength and stiffness, high crushing strength and very high resistance to shock. It is unsuitable for steam-bending.

Workability
Very difficult to work with hand tools, but can be tackled with machines. Has great resistance to cutting and a severe blunting effect. Pre-boring is required. Gluing has variable results.

Preservation
Very resistant to decay, insect and fungal attack, and is one of the

most durable woods in Africa. Very resistant to preservative treatment.

Uses
Heavy construction, marine work, mine shaft guides and so on. Also used as the running track for the rubber-wheeled trains of the Paris Métro. Check with your local environmental group or supplier before buying.

MICROBERLINIA BRAZZAVILLENSIS *FAMILY:* LEGUMINOSAE

Zebrano

Where it grows

This comes from two species, chiefly in Cameroons and Gabon. It is also known as zebrawood in the USA and UK.

Appearance

On quartered surfaces the heartwood has a light golden-yellow background, with veining of dark brown to almost black (giving its zebra appearance). The grain is interlocked or wavy and the texture is coarse with a lustrous surface.

Properties

Weight averages around 46 lb/ft^3. The wood is difficult to dry and is liable to distortion. It's stable in service, is high in all strength categories, and is noted for its very high stiffness. Not suitable for steam-bending.

Workability

Can be worked readily with hand and machine tools, but it is hard to obtain a smooth finish because of the grain. Care is required in gluing, and a clear filler should be used before polishing.

Preservation

It is non-durable and resistant to preservative treatment, but the sapwood is permeable.

Uses

Commonly supplied as sliced decorative veneers, and it is advisable to store them weighted down. In the solid, it is also used for turnery for small fancy items, and is used in sculpture and carving. Check with your local environmental group before buying.

MILLETTIA LAURENTII *FAMILY:* LEGUMINOSAE

Wengé and Panga-panga

Where it grows

Wengé occurs mainly in Zaire, Cameroons and Gabon, while the closely related species producing panga-panga occurs in Mozambique.

Appearance

The sapwood is whitish, clearly defined from the heartwood; this is dark brown, with close black veining and bands of light and dark tissue, producing a decorative figure. It is straight-grained with an irregular coarse texture.

Properties

Wengé weighs 52-62 lb/ft^3 and panga-panga 50 lb/ft^3. Both dry slowly and need care to avoid surface checking, but degrade is minimal. It is stable in service. Wengé has high bending strength and resistance to shock, and medium stiffness, with a poor steam-bending rating.

Workability

This durable wood works readily with hand and machine tools, but cutters should be kept sharp. Requires pre-boring for nailing and screwing.

Preservation

The wood is durable and extremely resistant to preservative treatment.

Uses

Wengé is excellent for flooring where there is heavy pedestrian traffic. Also used for interior and exterior joinery and general construction. Makes good turnery wood and is ideal for wood sculpture. Is sliced for veneers. Check with your local environmental group or supplier before buying.

4
2

6

4
4
6
H

MITRAGYNA CILIATA *FAMILY:* RUBIACEAE

Abura

Where it grows
It occurs in the wet coastal swamp forests of tropical West Africa from Sierra Leone and Liberia to Cameroons and Gabon.

Appearance
The sapwood is plain and not clearly defined from the heartwood, which varies between pale yellow and light brown. Grain is mostly straight, sometimes interlocked, and occasionally spiral. The texture is moderately fine and very even.

Properties
Weight varies from 29-43 lb/ft^3, averaging 34 lb/ft^3. It air- and kiln-dries rapidly and well, is very stable with small movement in service when dry, has very low stiffness, medium crushing strength and low shock resistance, with a very poor steam-bending classification.

Workability
Works well and cleanly with hand and machine tools, but is sometimes siliceous (contains silica) and this causes moderate to severe blunting. Cutting edges must be kept sharp. Pre-boring is advised for nailing and screwing.

Preservation
It is perishable and liable to insect attack, but the sapwood is permeable.

Uses
Very good for moldings, used for interior joinery and furniture framings, edge lippings, drawer sides; good for hardwearing flooring. Specialist uses include pattern making and vehicle bodywork. It is also cut for plywood and sliced for veneers. Check with your local environmental group before buying.

4
6
8
6
6
8
H

NAUCLEA DLIDERRICHII *FAMILY:* RUBIACEAE

Opepe

Where it grows
It occurs in the equatorial forests of West Africa – Guinea, Liberia, Ivory Coast, Ghana, Nigeria, and Cameroons.

Appearance
The creamy-pink sapwood is clearly demarcated from the heartwood, which is a distinctive golden-yellow, maturing to a uniform orange-brown. Sometimes straight-grained, but usually interlocked. The texture is coarse.

Properties
Weight averages about 46 lb/ft^3. Quarter-sawn material dries fairly quickly with very little checking or distortion. Flat-sawn wood is more refractory. It shows small movement in service, has medium bending strength and stiffness, high crushing strength and low shock resistance, with a poor steam-bending classification.

Workability
Works moderately well with hand and machine tools; quartered surfaces require a reduced cutting angle for planing. Pre-boring is advised for nailing and screwing.

Preservation
The heartwood has a high resistance to marine borers and fungi. The sapwood is liable to insect attack but is permeable for preservation treatment.

Uses
Exterior construction and marine work; also for interior joinery, furniture, cabinets, store fittings, turnery. Sliced for veneers. Check with your local environmental group before buying.

NESOGORDONIA PAPAVERIFERA *FAMILY:* TILIACEAE

Danta

color. It has a narrowly interlocked grain; the texture is fine.

Properties
Weight averages about 46 lb/ft^3. The wood dries well with little degrade, has medium movement in service, high bending and crushing strengths, low stiffness, and medium resistance to shock, with a moderate steam-bending rating.

Workability
Works easily with machine and hand tools, but will pick up on quartered surfaces. Requires pre-boring for screwing and nailing.

Preservation
Is liable to attack by the powder post beetle, and the heartwood is durable to marine borers.

Uses
Widely used for furniture, cabinet-making, interior and exterior joinery, store fittings, and bench tops; ideal for decorative flooring. Specialist uses include etching timber for graphic art, turnery for tool handles, stylish rifle and gunstocks. Selected logs are sliced for veneers. Check with your local environmental group or supplier before buying.

Where it grows
Danta occurs in the mixed deciduous forests of southern Nigeria, Ivory Coast, and Ghana.

Appearance
The sapwood is very pale brown with a pinkish tinge, clearly defined from the heartwood, which is a dark reddish-brown mahogany

NOTHOFAGUS CUNNINGHAMII *FAMILY:* FAGACEAE

Tasmanian Myrtle

often wavy, with a very fine, uniform, even texture.

Properties
Weight averages 45 lb/ft^3. The outer zone of lighter wood dries readily and well, but the inner zone is liable to honeycombing, severe internal checking and collapse, but this can be restored by reconditioning. It has small movement in service, a medium bending strength and stiffness, high crushing strength, and low resistance to shock, with a good steam-bending rating.

Workability
Works readily with both hand and machine tools, with moderate

blunting effect. Good holding properties for nailing and screwing, glues satisfactorily.

Preservation
The heartwood is non-durable and the sapwood is liable to attack by the powder post beetle, but is permeable for preservation treatment.

Uses
Very versatile, appears in cabinets and furniture, interior joinery and moldings, domestic flooring and parquetry blocks; also used for turning, food containers, vehicle bodywork; cut for plywood and sliced for veneers.

Where it grows
This Australian wood, closely related to northern hemisphere beech, occurs in Tasmania and Victoria.

Appearance
The pink to reddish-brown inner heartwood is separated from the narrow white sapwood by a zone of intermediate color. Grain is straight to slightly interlocked,

NOTHOFAGUS MENZIESII *FAMILY:* FAGACEAE

Silver Beech

Where it grows
These New Zealand trees are also known as Southland beech, red beech, and hard (or clinker) beech. They are not true beeches.

Appearance
The inner heartwood is a uniform pink-brown; there is a narrow sapwood and an intermediate zone of salmon-pink false heartwood (commercially regarded as sapwood) separating them. It is mostly straight-grained, sometimes curly, with a fine, even texture.

Properties
Silver beech weighs 33-46 lb/ft³, while red beech weighs 44 lb/ft³ and hard beech 48 lb/ft³. Dries fairly easily with a tendency to end splitting, but distortion is comparatively slight. It shows small movement in service, has medium bending and crushing strengths, low stiffness and resistance to shock loads, and a good steam-bending classification.

Workability
Silver and red work easily with hand and machine tools, except where irregular grain is present on quartered stock. Silica in hard beech causes severe dulling of edges.

Preservation
Silver is non-durable, but red and hard are both durable. They are liable to attack by the common furniture beetle and the powder post beetle. They are all extremely resistant to preservative treatment.

Uses
Cabinets, furniture, joinery, flooring, turnery; are cut for plywood and veneers.

OCHROMA PYRAMIDALE *FAMILY:* BOMBACACEAE

Balsa

Where it grows
It occurs from Cuba to Trinidad and from southern Mexico through Central America to Brazil. The bulk of the world's lightest wood comes from Ecuador, and supplies also come from India and Indonesia.

Appearance
Most commercial wood is the sapwood, which is white to oatmeal, often with a pinkish or yellow tinge. The central core of heartwood is pale brown. It is straight-grained, the texture fine, even and lustrous.

Properties
Weight ranges between 5-16 lb/ft³, averaging 10 lb/ft³. It's very difficult to dry and should be converted immediately after it is felled. Balsa is the weakest of all commercial timbers in all categories, and has a very poor steam-bending rating.

Workability
Easy to work with both hand and machine, thin-edged tools. Gluing is the best way to fasten balsa.

Preservation
It is perishable and liable to insect attack, but is permeable for preservation treatment.

Uses
Insulation in refrigerated ships, cold stores and so on. Prized for buoyancy in life-belts, rafts, floats, buoys, and water-sports equipment. Also good for modeling and theater props; and for corestock in laminated aircraft floors and partitions.

Where it grows

Stinkwood occurs in South Africa, from the forested country of the Cape Peninsula, northward to Natal and eastern Transvaal.

Appearance

The heartwood varies from a straw shade of gray-brown, through a dark reddish-brown, maturing to black. Grain varies from straight to

OCOTEA BULLATA *FAMILY:* LAURACEAE

Stinkwood

interlocked or spiral. It has an unpleasant odor when freshly worked, but this doesn't persist when it's dried.

Properties

Weight varies from 42 lb/ft³ for the light type to around 50 lb/ft³ for the darker types. The dark wood is more difficult to dry. It shows considerable shrinkage in service, has medium bending and crushing strengths and stiffness, and high resistance to shock. It is not used for steam-bending.

Workability

Works fairly easily with both hand and machine tools, but causes

severe blunting. Requires pre-boring for nailing and screwing, but glues without difficulty.

Uses

Highly prized in South Africa for high-class cabinets and furniture, especially Dutch designs of period furniture. Also used for light structural work and interior joinery, light domestic flooring, vehicle bodies; used for turnery and has some specialist uses, including ladders, sports goods, wheelwrighting, toys. Also sliced for veneers.

Where it grows

It grows in Kenya on the southern and eastern slopes of Mount Kenya and in the Aberdare range. In Tanzania it occurs on Mount Kilimanjaro, Usambara, and Upare.

Appearance

The sapwood is not clearly defined from the heartwood, which is light yellow to greenish-brown, maturing into a deep brown. Many trees are

OCOTEA USAMBARENSIS *FAMILY:* LAURACEAE

East African Camphorwood

ill-shaped with twisted or interlocked grain, the texture moderately fine.

Properties

Weight varies from 32-40 lb/ft³, averaging about 37 lb/ft³. The wood dries slowly if kiln-dried, with little degrade, but may warp if air-dried too quickly. Is stable in service, has medium bending and crushing strengths, low stiffness, and low resistance to shock, with a moderately good steam-bending rating.

Workability

Works well with hand and machine tools with only slight dulling, but the interlocked grain affects

machining operations. Takes nails satisfactorily, glues well, stains easily and produces an excellent finish.

Preservation

Very durable, resistant to insect attack and extremely resistant to preservative treatment, but the sapwood is permeable.

Uses

Ideal for clothes closets; is also used for cabinets, furniture, interior and exterior joinery, light construction, vehicles, flooring. Sliced for veneers. Check with your local environmental group or supplier before buying.

9

10

10

10
10
10
10
H

OCOTEA RODIAEI *FAMILY:* LAURACEAE

Greenheart

Where it grows

This is the major commercial wood of Guyana, and occurs to a limited extent in Surinam and Venezuela.

Appearance

The pale yellow-green sapwood shades gradually into the heartwood, which varies from yellow-green through olive to dark brown, and is often marked with black streaks. Grain varies from straight to interlocked, texture is fine, uniform, and lustrous.

Properties

Weight averages 64 lb/ft^3. It dries slowly with considerable degrade, has medium movement in service,

has exceptional strength in all categories, with a moderate steam-bending rating.

Workability

Moderately difficult and dangerous to work as poisonous splinters fly from interlocked, cross- or endgrain; the difficult grain also affects machining. Pre-boring is essential. Gluing results are variable. A lustrous surface can be obtained.

Preservation

Greenheart is very durable and immune to marine borers, and is extremely resistant to preservative treatment.

Uses

Marine and ship construction of all kinds, heavy-duty factory flooring, chemical vats; also turnery of all kinds, pool and billiard cue butts, fishing rods, and the central laminae of longbows. Check with your local environmental group before buying.

8

8

8

10
9
8
8
H

OLEA HOCHSTETTERI *FAMILY:* OLEACEAE

Olivewood

Where it grows

It is grown in the Mediterranean for its edible fruit and olive oil, and commercial wood comes from Kenya, Tanzania, and Uganda.

Appearance

The sapwood is pale creamy-yellow and quite plain, but the heartwood has a pale brown background with attractive markings. Grain is straight to shallowly interlocked and the texture very fine and even.

Properties

Varies from 50-55 lb/ft^3 in weight, is rather refractory and needs to be air-dried slowly; can be kiln-dried successfully. It shows considerable

movement in service, has excellent strength in every category. Sapwood may be bent to a small radius, but olivewood has only a moderate steam-bending classification.

Workability

Rather difficult to work as the interlocked grain affects machining. There's high resistance in cutting, with moderate blunting. Requires pre-boring.

Preservation

The heartwood is moderately durable and resistant to preservative treatment, but the sapwood is permeable.

Uses

Excellent for decorative flooring for public buildings; also used for furniture, cabinets, and paneling and is ideal for turnery. Olivewood is popular for sculpture and carving and is sliced for veneers.

PALAQUIUM AND PAYENA SPP. *FAMILY:* SAPOTACEAE

Nyatoh

Where it grows
Certain species, producing woods of similar colors and properties from Malaysia, Indonesia, and the south Asian islands are collectively known as nyatoh.

Appearance
Generally, the sapwood is only slightly paler and not defined from the heartwood, which is a deep

pink to red-brown, often with darker streaks on quartered surfaces. Grain can be straight, slightly interlocked, or slightly wavy; texture is moderately fine and even.

Properties
Weight averages 40-45 lb/ft^3. The wood dries slowly with a slight tendency to end split and distort; is stable in service and has medium bending and crushing strength, with low stiffness and resistance to shock, and a moderate steam-bending rating.

Workability
Some species are siliceous and can cause severe blunting. Pre-boring is required for nailing, but the wood

glues well and can be brought to an excellent finish.

Preservation
Sapwood liable to attack by the powder post beetle and the heartwood varies from non-durable to moderately durable. It is very resistant to preservative treatment.

Uses
The name covers several different woods, but generally they're attractive timbers for cabinet-making, furniture, pattern-making, interior constructions, high-class joinery; also for plywood and veneers. Check with your local environmental group before buying.

6
6
7
6
6
6
6
H

PARATECOMA PEROBA *FAMILY:* BIGNONACEAE

White Peroba

Where it grows
The tree grows in the coastal forests of Brazil.

Appearance
The white to yellowish sapwood is clearly defined from the heartwood, which is a pale golden-olive brown, but with yellow, greenish or red shading. Grain is commonly interlocked or wavy, and the

texture medium and uniform, often with a lustrous surface.

Properties
Weight averages about 47 lb/ft^3, and the wood dries easily. It shows medium movement in service, has a medium bending strength, low stiffness and shock resistance, and high crushing strength, with a moderate steam-bending classification.

Workability
Works readily with hand and machine tools, and planes easily to a smooth, silken finish. Has good holding properties, glues well, and can be brought to a good finish.

Preservation
The durable heartwood resists insect and fungal attacks, and is also resistant to preservative treatment.

Uses
High-class furniture and cabinet-making, especially in Brazil; also for interior and exterior joinery and in building construction; good for heavy-duty flooring, vehicle bodywork, decking, and vats for foodstuffs. Is sliced for veneers. Check with your local environmental group before buying.

4
4
8
6
8
8
8
H

PELTOGYNE SPP. *FAMILY:* LEGUMINOSAE

Purpleheart

Where it grows
Purpleheart is widely distributed in tropical America from Mexico down to southern Brazil.

Appearance
It has a white to cream sapwood; heartwood, bright purple on exposure, matures to a dark purplish brown. Generally straight-grained, but sometimes wavy or · interlocked with a moderate to fine, uniform texture.

Properties
Weight averages about 54 lb/ft^3. It dries fairly rapidly with little degrade, has little movement in service, has high bending and crushing strength and stiffness, with medium resistance to shock, and a moderate steam-bending rating.

Workability
Rather difficult to work, with a moderate to severe blunting effect on tools; requires pre-boring, but flues well. Spirit finishes tend to remove the purple color.

Preservation
The permeable sapwood is liable to insect attack; the heartwood is very durable and extremely resistant to preservative treatment.

Uses
Used locally as a cabinet and furniture wood, but also for heavy outdoor constructional work; also for carving and sculpture, turnery; boats, gym apparatus, diving boards, skis, wheelwrighting, pool-cue butts; is also sliced for veneers. Check with your local environmental group before buying.

PERICOPSIS ELATA *FAMILY:* LEGUMINOSAE

Afrormosia

Where it grows
This tree occurs in the Ivory Coast, Ghana, Zaire, and Nigeria. It is also known in its various regions as assamela, kokrodua, ayin, egbi, and andejen.

Appearance
The creamy-buff sapwood is well defined from the heartwood, which is golden-brown when freshly felled, and darkens on exposure. The grain varies from straight to interlocked, the texture is moderately fine.

Properties
Weighs about 43 lb/ft^3 and dries slowly but with little degrade. It shows exceptionally small movement in service, has medium stiffness, high crushing strength, and medium shock resistance, with a moderate steam-bending rating.

Workability
The interlocked grain can affect machining and tipped saws should be used; pre-boring is required, but it glues well and takes a good finish.

Preservation
Is very durable, resistant to both fungi and termites, and extremely resistant to preservative treatment.

Uses
It appears in high-class furniture and cabinet-making, chairs, interior joinery, stairs, store and office fittings and, agricultural implements. Also used for boat building and marine piling; and is sliced for decorative veneers for furniture, flush doors and wall paneling. Check with your local environmental group before buying.

Where it grows
This grows in southern Brazil. It is also known as imbuya, amarela, canella imbuia, and embuia (Brazil); or Brazilian walnut in the USA and UK.

Appearance
The beige sapwood is clearly defined from the heartwood, which varies from olive-yellow to

PHOEBE POROSA *FAMILY:* LAURACEAE

Imbuia

chocolate, and is frequently variegated. Grain may be straight but sometimes wavy or curly, with a fine to medium texture and high luster.

Properties
Weighs about 41 lb/ft^3, air-dries rapidly – but care is needed to avoid warp. It should be kiln-dried slowly to avoid degrade. It exhibits small movement in service, has medium to low strength in all categories, with a very low steam-bending classification.

Workability
Works easily with hand and machine tools, with only slight blunting, and finishes very

smoothly. Has good holding properties, glues without problems, stains and polishes easily and takes a good finish.

Preservation
The durable heartwood resists insect attack and is moderately resistant to preservative treatment, but the sapwood is permeable.

Uses
High-class cabinet and furniture work, superior interior joinery for paneling, store and bank fitting; also makes high-grade decorative flooring for light use. Check with your local environmental group before buying.

5
5
6
6
5
7
H

Where it grows
This occurs throughout Europe, with the exception of Denmark and the Netherlands, and into western Russia.

Appearance
Color varies from almost white to pale yellow-brown, and has a natural luster. The annual rings are clearly defined. The wood is

PICEA ABIES *FAMILY:* PINACEAE

Spruce, European or Whitewood

straight-grained and has a fine texture.

Properties
Weight averages 29 lb/ft^3. Spruce dries rapidly with some risk of distortion. It has medium movement in service, low stiffness and resistance to shock, medium bending and crushing strength, and a very poor steam-bending rating.

Workability
Works easily with hand and machine tools, holds screws and nails well, glues satisfactorily and takes stain, paint and varnishes to a good finish.

Preservation
The sapwood is liable to attack by the common furniture beetle; the non-durable heartwood is resistant to preservative treatment.

Uses
As well as providing our Christmas trees, it is used for interior building work, carcassing, domestic flooring, general carpentry, boxes, and crates. Spruce from central and eastern Europe and from Alpine areas of North America produce excellent "tone woods" for keyboard instruments. Is also used for plywood.

4
4
5
3
5
5
S

PICEA SITCHENSIS *FAMILY:* PINACEAE

Sitka Spruce

Where it grows
This occurs on the Pacific coast of North America and western Canada down to California.

Appearance
The pale pink sapwood blends into the light pinkish-brown heartwood, which is mostly straight-grained, sometimes spiral. It has a fairly coarse but uniform texture.

Properties
Weighs about 27 lb/ft^3 and care is needed in drying large sizes, as it dries fairly rapidly and tends to twist and cup. It has medium movement in service, has medium bending and crushing strengths, stiffness, and shock resistance; and its strength-to-weight ratio is high. It has a good steam-bending rating.

Workability
Works easily with hand and machine tools, finishes cleanly, takes screws and nails easily, and gives good results with various finishes.

Preservation
The heartwood is non-durable and resistant to preservative treatment.

Uses
Strength varies, so selective grading is necessary for joists, rafters, and studding for buildings. Split poles are used for ladder sides. In Canada, it is used for interior joinery, cooperage and boxmaking; specialized uses include boats, oars, and masts, while some grades make soundboards for pianos, guitars, and violins. It is also the most important pulp for newsprint.

PINUS MONTICOLA *FAMILY:* PINACEAE

Western White Pine

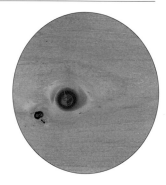

Where it grows
It grows in the mountain forests of western Canada and the western USA, and south down to the Kern River in California and east into northern Montana; it is most abundant in northern Idaho.

Appearance
The sapwood is white, the heartwood only slightly darker, varying from pale straw to shades of reddish-brown. It is straight-grained with an even, uniform texture.

Properties
Weighs around 28 lb/ft^3, dries readily and well with little checking or warping. It shows little movement in service, has rather low strength properties, and is not suitable for steam-bending.

Workability
Works easily with machine and hand tools, takes screws and nails without difficulty, and takes paint and varnish well.

Preservation
The wood is non-durable, liable to beetle attack, and is moderately resistant to preservative treatment; the sapwood is permeable.

Uses
Used chiefly for interior joinery for doors and windows, interior trim, fitments, shelving, light and medium building construction; also for furniture and cabinets, boats and ships, pattern-making, drawing boards. It is cut for plywood and sliced for paneling veneers.

PINUS PALUSTRIS *FAMILY:* PINACEAE

American Pitch Pine

Where it grows
This is the heaviest commercial softwood and grows through the southern US in a curve from Virginia through Florida to the Gulf.

Appearance
The creamy-pink sapwood is quite narrow, and contrasts with the heartwood, which is yellow-red to reddish brown with a conspicuous growth-ring figure. It is resinous and has a coarse texture.

Properties
Weighs from 41-43 lb/ft^3 and dries well with little degrade. It is stable in service, has high bending and crushing strengths and high stiffness, with medium resistance to shock. Not suitable for steam-bending.

Workability
Can be worked readily with both hand and machine tools, but resin can be troublesome. Holds screws and nails firmly, glues well and takes finishes satisfactorily.

Preservation
It is moderately durable; sometimes beetle damage is present. It is resistant to preservative treatment, but the sapwood is permeable.

Uses
Heavy construction work, trucks and railroad trucks, shipbuilding, exterior joinery, piling, dock work, bridges, decking and chemical vats; lower grades are used for interior joinery, domestic flooring, crates, etc.

PINUS PONDEROSA *FAMILY:* PINACEAE

Ponderosa Pine

Where it grows
This occurs in the drier regions of southern British Columbia and from Montana, western Nebraska, and Texas into Mexico and west to the Pacific coast.

Appearance
Mature trees have a very thick pale yellow sapwood, soft, non-resinous and uniform texture. Heartwood is orange to reddish-brown and is occasionally heavier than sapwood.

Properties
Weighs about 32 lb/ft^3 and dries easily and well with little degrade. It shows little movement in service, has medium bending and crushing strength, low stiffness and shock resistance, and a poor steam-bending rating.

Workability
Works well with hand and machine tools but resin tends to clog cutters and saws. Can be glued satisfactorily, takes screws and nails well and, after removal of surface gumminess, gives good results with painting and varnishing.

Preservation
It is non-durable and moderately resistant to preservative treatment, but the sapwood is permeable.

Uses
The sapwood is used in America for pattern-making; the heartwood is used for kitchen furniture, building construction, window frames, doors, general carpentry, and for packing cases, crates and pallets. Logs are cut for veneers and knotty pine paneling.

PINUS RADIATA *FAMILY:* PINACEAE

Radiata Pine

Where it grows

This is the most commonly planted softwood in the warm temperate climates of California, Australia, New Zealand, and South Africa.

Appearance

Most commercial lumber has wide pale sapwood and a rather small, pinkish-brown heartwood with inconspicuous growth rings, giving an even, uniform texture. Grain is usually straight, sometimes spiral.

Properties

Weighs about 30 lb/ft^3 and dries rapidly and well with little degrade, and is stable in use. It has low bending strength and stiffness, with medium crushing strength and shock resistance; it is not suitable for steam-bending.

Workability

Works fairly well with both hand and machine tools and holds screws and nails well. Gluing and finishing are satisfactory.

Preservation

Is non-durable and there is sometimes beetle damage. The sapwood is liable to attack by the common furniture beetle, but is permeable for preservation treatment.

Uses

Mainly for building and general structural purposes; also boxes, packing cases, and crates; general turnery for broom handles and the like; furniture and interior joinery. Selected logs produce plywood and veneers.

PINUS STROBUS *FAMILY:* PINACEAE

Northern Pine

Where it grows

This species occurs from Newfoundland to the Manitoba border and south to north Georgia. It is also known as white pine, eastern white, cork and soft pine (Canada and USA), northern white, Yellow pine (USA), Quebec yellow, Quebec pine and Weymouth pine (UK).

Appearance

The sapwood is white and the heartwood varies from light straw-brown to light reddish brown. It is straight-grained and the texture is fine and even.

Properties

Weighs 24-26 lb/ft^3 and dries fairly rapidly and well. It has extremely low shrinkage and is very stable in service, is weak in all strength properties and is not suitable for steam-bending.

Workability

Works very easily with hand and machine tools.

Preservation

It's susceptible to attack by the common furniture beetle. Heartwood is non-durable and resistant to preservative treatment, but the sapwood is permeable to treatment.

Uses

Well suited to engineers' pattern-making as well as drawing boards, doors and similar high-class work; also used for sculpture, carving, and interior joinery, cabinet and furniture work; specialist uses include parts for musical instruments.

PINUS SYLVESTRIS *FAMILY:* PINACEAE

Redwood

Where it grows
This common commercial softwood occurs from the Sierra Nevada in Andalusia and the mountains of west Spain, through the Maritime Alps and Pyrenees, the Caucasus and Transylvanian Alps, up into western Siberia.

Appearance
The knotty wood has a mildly resinous heartwood of pale red-brown, distinct from the paler sapwood. Texture varies from fine to coarse, depending on where it grows.

Properties
Weighs about 32 lb/ft³ and dries well with a tendency to blue sap stain. It shows medium movement in service, has low stiffness and resistance to shock, low to medium bending and crushing strength and a very poor steam-bending rating.

Workability
Works easily with hand and machine tools, holds nails and screws well, and can be well finished.

Preservation
It's liable to attack by the common furniture beetle, is non-durable and moderately resistant to preservative treatment; but the sapwood is permeable.

Uses
Best grades are used for furniture, interior joinery, turnery and vehicle bodies; other grades for building construction and carcassing. When treated it is used for railroad sleepers, telephone poles, piles and mine props. Logs are cut for plywood and veneers.

4
4
6
3
5
5
S

PIRATINERA GUIANENSIS *FAMILY:* MORACEAE

Snakewood

Where it grows
Many species of *Piratinera* occur in central and tropical South America, from the Amazon region of Brazil through Guyana, Venezuela, Colombia, and Panama, Southern Mexico and the West Indies. Commercial supplies come from Guyana, French Guiana and Surinam, with smaller quantities from Brazil, Bolivia, and Trinidad.

Also known as Leopard wood (USA) and letterwood (UK).

Appearance
This is one of the most expensive woods in the world and gets its name from its red to reddish-brown snakeskin appearance. It is irregular grained, but the texture is moderately fine.

Properties
Weighs about 31 lb/ft³ and is very hard when air-dried. It's difficult to dry and undergoes some degrade. It shows medium movement in service, and is exceptionally strong in all categories, and is not suitable for steam-bending.

Workability
Very difficult to work, with severe blunting. Care is needed in gluing and finishing.

Preservation
Very durable and immune to insect attack, and extremely resistant to preservation treatment.

Uses
Superb for turnery, walking sticks, drumsticks, fishing-rod butts, and fancy handles. Also used for violin bows and is the traditional wood for native archery bows. Also used for veneers. Check with your local environmental group or supplier before buying.

9
8
10
9
10
9
H

PLATANUS HYBRIDA *FAMILY:* PLATANACEAE

European Plane

Where it grows
It occurs throughout Europe. The related species, *P. orientalis*, produces eastern plane tree, which occurs in south-east Europe, Turkey, and Iran. *P. occidentalis* produces American plane, known as sycamore or buttonwood in the USA.

Appearance
The sapwood is not very distinct from the heartwood, which is light reddish-brown with darker broad rays on quartered material. It is straight-grained with a fine to medium texture.

Properties
Weighs on average 39 lb/ft^3, and air-dries fairly rapidly, is prone to splitting, and has a tendency to distort. It is stable in service, has medium strength in all categories except for low stiffness, which earns it a very good steam-bending rating.

Workability
Works well with hand and machine tools, and has only moderate blunting. Sharp cutters are required when planing, and there's a tendency to bind on saws.

Preservation
The sapwood is liable to attack by the common furniture beetle; the heartwood is perishable but permeable to preservation treatment.

Uses
Interiors of high-class cabinets and furniture, joinery, carriage interiors, light construction, door skins and paneling; and in turnery for striking handles. Also produces veneers.

PODOCARPUS SPP. *FAMILY:* PODOCARPACEAE

Podo

Where it grows
Several species grow chiefly in Central America, East Africa, and Asia.

Appearance
There is a very slight distinction between the sapwood and the heartwood, which is light yellow-brown. It has a uniform texture and is straight-grained.

Properties
Weighs between 32-39 lb/ft^3, and dries fairly rapidly, with a pronounced tendency to distort. It shows medium movement in service, has medium bending and crushing strengths, very low stiffness, low resistance to shock, and a moderate steam-bending rating.

Workability
Works easily with both hand and machine tools, but is brittle. Requires pre-boring for nailing, but holds screws well and glues satisfactorily. Doesn't take stain uniformly.

Preservation
Is liable to insect attack and is non-durable, but is permeable for preservation treatment.

Uses
Podo is used where durability is not of major importance for joinery and interior fittings in building construction, scaffold planks and boards, fascia boards, flooring and framing, kitchen furniture, and moldings. Also used for turnery and, when treated, for weatherboards and boat-building. Makes good-quality plywood and is sliced for veneers. Check with your local environmental group or supplier before buying.

2

2

4

4

4

6

S

PODOCARPUS TOTARA *FAMILY:* PODOCARPACEAE

Totara

Where it grows
This occurs only in New Zealand.

Appearance
It is a straight-grained wood of medium reddish-brown with a fairly fine, even texture. Growth rings are not clearly defined.

Properties
Weighs 30 lb/ft^3, dries fairly rapidly with little degrade, and exhibits small movement in service. It has low bending strength and resistance to shock, but medium crushing strength, making it more suitable for columns than beams.

Workability
Works easily with both hand and machine tools. This species and *P. hallii* hold screws and nails well, but care is needed in gluing and the resin content needs special treatment before painting.

Preservation
The wood has natural durability and a high resistance to decay, but is liable to attack by the common furniture beetle. The heartwood is resistant to preservative treatment, but the sapwood is permeable.

Uses
A very important wood in New Zealand for docks, wharf and harbor work because it is the only softwood resistant to attack by marine borers; also used in ships and boats and for chemical vats; also for flooring, cladding, and shingles. It is the traditional wood for Maori carvings and canoes.

6

6

8

8

8

8

8

H

POMETIA PINNATA *FAMILY:* SAPINDACEAE

Taun

Where it grows
It occurs widely throughout the South Pacific, and its names include kasai, awa, ako, malagai, and agupanga.

Appearance
The pink sapwood is not demarcated from the heartwood, which is a pale pinkish-brown maturing to a dull red-brown.

Usually straight-grained, sometimes interlocked or wavy.

Properties
Weighs on average 42-46 lb/ft^3 and needs care in drying to avoid warping and splitting. It shows medium movement in service, has high bending and crushing strengths, medium stiffness and resistance to shock, and a good steam-bending rating.

Workability
Works readily with both hand and machine tools, with only a moderate blunting of edges. Holds screws and nails well, glues satisfactorily, takes stain well and finishes well.

Preservation
It is moderately durable, and resistant to preservation treatment.

Uses
Widely used in the Philippines in constructional work; also used for exterior joinery, door and window frames, boat planking and framing, wharf decking, capstan bars, masts, and spars. In Australia it is used for furniture and cabinets, pianos and, as turnery wood, for bobbins, handles and fancy goods. Is cut for plywood and veneer. Check with your local environmental group before buying.

POPULUS TREMULOIDES *FAMILY:* SALICACEAE

Canadian Aspen

Where it grows
This is one of the most widely distributed trees in North America.

Appearance
The sapwood is not distinct from the heartwood, which is cream-white to very pale cookie. Mostly straight-grained, occasionally wavy and inclined to be woolly. Texture is fine and even.

Properties
Weighs on average 28 lb/ft^3, dries easily, but is inclined to warp and twist in drying, and distort unless care is taken in piling. It shows small movement in service, has low bending and crushing strengths, low stiffness, medium resistance to shock, and a very poor steam-bending rating.

Workability
Works easily with hand and machine tools but will tear and bind on the saw; very sharp, thin-edged tools are needed. It holds screws and nails easily and glues well, but staining may be patchy on woolly surfaces.

Preservation
It is non-durable and extremely resistant to preservative treatment.

Uses
Has a wide range of uses: furniture interiors and fitments, brake blocks for iron wheels, vehicle bodies, the bottoms of trucks; food containers, fruit baskets, packing cases – to name a few.

POPULUS SPP. *FAMILY:* SALICACEAE

Poplar

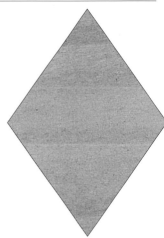

Where it grows
To be found widely in northern temperate regions.

Appearance
The heartwood, not clearly defined from the sapwood, varies from cream-white to very pale straw and in some species to pale brown or pink-brown. It is usually straight-grained and rather woolly, but with a fine, even texture.

Properties
Weighs on average 28 lb/ft^3 and dries fairly rapidly and well with little degrade. It exhibits medium movement in service, has low bending strength, very low stiffness and shock resistance, medium crushing strength, and a very poor steam-bending rating.

Workability
Works easily with hand and machine tools, but very sharp, thin-edged cutters are required. Holds screws and nails well but staining can be patchy.

Preservation
Logs are liable to attack by beetles and wood boring caterpillars (*Cossidae*). The sapwood, which constitutes a large proportion of the tree, is perishable but permeable for preservation treatment.

Uses
Interior joinery, furniture, framing, toys, and turnery. Logs are cut for plywood and corestock, and sliced for veneers.

PRUNUS SPP. *FAMILY:* ROSACEAE

Cherry

Appearance
The creamy-pink sapwood of the European species is clearly defined from the heartwood, which is a pale pinkish-brown, maturing to red-brown. The North American version is a darker red-brown. Both have straight grain and a fairly fine, even texture.

Properties
Weighs 36-38 lb/ft^3, dries fairly rapidly with a tendency to warp and shrink. It shows medium movement in service, has medium bending and crushing strengths and resistance to shock, low stiffness, and a very good steam-bending rating.

Workability
Works well with hand and machine tools, with moderate blunting; and cross-grained wood tends to tear in planing. It holds screws and nails well, and finishes excellently.

Preservation
Moderately durable; sapwood is prone to the common furniture beetle, but almost immune to the powder post beetle. Heartwood is moderately durable and resistant to preservative treatment.

Uses
Furniture, cabinets, carving, sculpture, and, among other things, parts for musical instruments.

Where it grows
The European species produces European Cherry, known as wild cherry in the UK. American Cherry, also known as black cherry in Canada and the USA and cabinet cherry in the USA occurs from Ontario to Florida, and from the Dakotas to Texas.

PSEUDOTSUGA MENZIESII *FAMILY:* PINACEAE

Douglas Fir

Appearance
The sapwood is slightly lighter than the heartwood, which is a light reddish-brown. There's a prominent growth-ring figure. Grain is mostly straight, and texture is medium and uniform.

Properties
Weighs 33 lb/ft^3 and dries fairly rapidly and well, without much warping, but knots tend to split and loosen. It is stable in service, has high bending strength, stiffness, and crushing strength, medium resistance to shock, and a poor steam-bending rating.

Workability
Works readily with both hand and machine tools, but cutters should be kept very sharp, as there's moderate blunting.

Preservation
Subject to beetle attack, is moderately durable, and resistant to preservation treatment.

Uses
This is the world's most important source of plywood. In the solid, it is used for heavy construction work, interior and exterior joinery, dock and harbor work, railroad sleepers and other heavy use.

Where it grows
Known as British Columbia pine or Columbian pine in the UK, and Oregon pine in the USA, this is not a true fir. It occurs in abundance in British Columbia, Washington and Oregon, through Wyoming to southern New Mexico and west to the Pacific coast.

PTEROCARPUS ANGOLENSIS *FAMILY:* LEGUMINOSAE

Muninga

Where it grows
This occurs in the savannah forests of Tanzania, Zambia, Angola, Mozambique, Zimbabwe, and South Africa.

Appearance
The oatmeal sapwood is clearly defined from the heartwood, which matures into deep golden brown with darker markings. Grain, usually straight, is sometimes irregularly interlocked, producing an attractive figure. Texture is fairly coarse and uneven.

Properties
Weighs on average 39 lb/ft^3 (the material from Zimbabwe is lighter). It has excellent drying properties and dries fairly slowly, with only a slight tendency to surface checking. It is exceptionally stable in use, has medium bending strength, very low stiffness, low shock resistance, a high crushing strength, and a high steam-bending classification.

Workability
Works easily with hand and machine tools, but with a tendency for the irregular grain to pick up when planing. Good holding properties; glues well.

Preservation
The sapwood is liable to attack by the powder post beetle. The heartwood is very durable and resistant to preservative treatment.

Uses
Excellent for turnery and is also used for carving and sculpture, high-class joinery and, in solid and veneer forms, for furniture, cabinets, and paneling. Also makes excellent flooring. Check with your local environmental group or supplier before buying.

PTEROCARPUS SOYAUXII *FAMILY:* LEGUMINOSAE

African Padauk

Where it grows
This occurs in central and tropical West Africa, and is known as camwood or barwood in the UK.

Appearance
When freshly cut, the heartwood is a very distinctive, vivid blood red, maturing to dark purple-brown with red streaks – sharply demarcated from the straw-colored sapwood. The grain is straight to interlocked and the texture varies from moderate to very coarse.

Properties
Weighs 40-50 lb/ft^3 and dries very well with minimum degrade. It is very dense with high bending and crushing strengths and medium stiffness and resistance to shock, but it is not suitable for steam-bending. Very stable in service.

Workability
Works well with hand and machine tools with only a slight blunting. Holds nails and screws well, glues easily and can be finished well.

Preservation
The wood is very durable and renowned for resistance to decay. It is also moderately resistant to preservative treatment.

Uses
It is world-famous as a dye wood, but is also used for high-class cabinets, furniture, and interior joinery; excellent for turnery and for carving and sculpture. Specialized uses include electrical fittings and spirit levels. Check with your local environmental group or supplier before buying.

PTEROCARPUS INDICUS *FAMILY:* LEGUMINOSAE

Narra

Appearance
The light straw-colored sapwood is quite clearly defined from the valuable heartwood, which varies from golden-yellow to brick red. It produces a range of attractive figures, the texture is moderately fine and the grain is wavy and interlocked.

Properties
Weighs on average 41 lb/ft^3, but darker wood is heavier. It dries slowly but well, the red requiring more care than the yellow. It is stable in use, has medium strength in all categories.

Where it grows
It is known as red or yellow narra in the USA and occurs throughout southern and south-east Asia, producing Solomons padauk or Papua New Guinea rosewood. It is found extensively in the Philippines and is abundant in Cagayan, Mindoro, Palawan, and Cotabato.

Workability
Straight-grained wood works well with both hand and machine tools with only a slight dulling; irregular grain requires a reduced cutting angle. It takes screws and nails well and glues easily.

Preservation
It is resistant to fungal and insect attack, very durable, and resistant to preservative treatment.

Uses
Used locally for cabinets, furniture, and joinery; also for sculpture and carving, cases for scientific instruments, parts for musical instruments. Check with your local environmental group before buying.

PYRUS COMMUNIS *FAMILY:* ROSACEAE

Pear

Where it grows
There are numerous varieties. It originated in southern Europe and western Asia, but commercial lumber comes from Italy, Switzerland, France, Germany, and the Tyrol.

Appearance
The sapwood is pale yellow-apricot, and the heartwood varies from flesh tone to a pale pinkish-brown. Grain is straight, sometimes irregular, producing a handsome mottled figure.

Properties
Weight is 43-44 lb/ft^3 and pear dries slowly, but with a tendency to warp and distort where there's irregular gain. It is strong, tough, and stable in use, but its strength is unimportant because it is available in only small sizes. It is not used for steam-bending.

Workability
It machines well but is moderately hard to saw, and gives a high blunting effect. It glues well and gives excellent results with stain and polish.

Preservation
Pear is perishable, but permeable for impregnation.

Uses
It has excellent turning properties, and is used for fancy goods, wooden bowls, the backs and handles of brooms, umbrella handles, and drawing instruments such as set squares and T-squares. Also excellent for carving and sculpture, and for musical instruments such as recorders. It is also used for veneers.

QUERCUS SPP. *FAMILY:* FAGACEAE

American Red Oak

Where it grows
Grows in eastern Canada and northern USA, but is more prevalent in Canada. It is also found in Iran as Persian oak.

Appearance
It outwardly resembles the white oak, except that the heartwood varies from cookie-pinkish to reddish-brown. The grain is usually straight; southern red oak is coarser textured than northern.

Properties
Weighs on average 48 lb/ft^3, dries slowly, and care is needed in air and kiln drying to prevent degrade.

It exhibits medium movement in service, has medium bending strength and stiffness, high shock resistance and crushing strength, and a very good steam-bending rating.

Workability
Offers moderate blunting to cutters, which should be kept sharp. Requires pre-boring for nails and screws; gluing results are variable, but red oak takes stain well and polishes to a good finish.

Preservation
It's non-durable, moderately resistant to preservative treatment, and unsuited to exterior work.

Uses
Its use is limited by its lack of durability and drying problems, but it is good for domestic flooring, furniture fitments, interior joinery, and vehicle construction. Logs are cut for plywood, and sliced for veneers.

QUERCUS ALBA. *FAMILY:* FAGACEAE

White Oak

Where it grows
The genus *Quercus* produces more than 200 different species. Most white oaks occur in the temperate regions of the northern hemisphere.

Appearance
The sapwood is lighter than the heartwood, which is light tan or yellow-brown, usually straight-grained, but often irregular or cross-grained. It has a moderately coarse texture.

Properties
Weighs 45-47 lb/ft^3, while some, notably Volhynian, Slavonian, and Japanese, are lighter. It air-dries very slowly with a tendency to split

and check. These dense woods have high strength, low stiffness and resistance to shock, and a very good steam-bending rating.

Workability
They are corrosive to metals and liable to blue-stain in damp conditions. Machining is generally satisfactory, and they can be brought to an excellent finish.

Preservation
The wood is durable but liable to beetle attack; it is extremely resistant to preservative treatment, though the sapwood is permeable.

Uses
It is one of the world's most popular woods, used for furniture, cabinet-making, boat-building, dock and harbor work, vehicle bodywork, high-class interior and exterior joinery and flooring. Excellent for sculpture and carving, and also for tight cooperage for whiskey, sherry, and brandy casks. It is sliced for veneers.

SALIX SPP. *FAMILY:* SALICACEAE

Willow

Appearance
It has a white sapwood and a creamy-white heartwood, with a pink tinge. It is typically straight-grained, with a fine, even texture.

Properties
Weight averages 28 lb/ft^3, and the wood dries well and fairly rapidly, with minimal degrade. It is stable in use, has low bending and crushing strengths, very low stiffness and resistance to shock, and a poor steam-bending rating.

Workability
Works easily with hand and machine tools, with slight blunting; sharp cutters are needed to avoid woolliness. It takes nails, and glues well, and can be brought to an excellent stained finish.

Preservation
It is perishable and liable to attack by the powder post and common furniture beetles. It is resistant to preservation treatment, but the sapwood is permeable.

Uses
Selected butts of cricket-bat willow are used for cleft cricket-bat blades. Other willows are used for artificial limbs, clogs, flooring, brake blocks in colliery winding gear, toys, boxes, crates. It is sliced for moiré veneers.

Where it grows
The main commercial species occur in Europe, western Asia, North Africa, and the USA. *S. alba* produces white willow and common willow in the UK, and *S. nigra* produces black willow in the USA.

4

2

4

3

4

4

H

SCOTTELLIA SPP. *FAMILY:* FLACOURTIACEAE

Odoko

Properties
Weight averages 39 lb/ft^3, and the wood air-dries fairly rapidly, with a tendency to check and split, and is prone to staining. These woods have medium movement in service and medium bending strength, stiffness, and resistance to shock loads, with a high crushing strength and a poor steam-bending classification.

Workability
It is fairly easy to work by both hand and machine, with only slight blunting. Brittleness can cause chipping or flaking on quartered stock. It requires pre-boring for nailing, but glues well.

Preservation
These species are non-durable and prone to discoloration by staining fungi, but are permeable for preservative treatment.

Uses
Domestic woodware, furniture, fitments, interior joinery, and light construction. Also for carving, turnery, brushbacks, and shoe heels. It also makes excellent flooring, with a high resistance to wear. Also produces veneers and plywood. Check with your local environmental group or supplier before buying.

Where it grows
Several species occur in West Africa.

Appearance
The sapwood is not clearly defined from the heartwood, which is pale yellow to cookie with darker zones. Grain is generally straight, but sometimes interlocked, showing an attractive figure. Texture is fine, even and lustrous.

5

6

6

7

5

8

H

3
3
4
3
4
4
S

SEQUOIA SEMPERVIRENS *FAMILY:* TAXODIACEAE

Sequoia

Where it grows
The "big tree" of California, a protected species whose dimensions are unequalled, is the *Sequoia gigantea,* and its wood is of no commercial use. Its cousin *S. sempervirens,* produces the sequoia, known as the Californian redwood in the UK and USA. It occurs in southern Oregon and northern California, and reaches 340 ft with a diameter of 10-15 ft.

Appearance
The sapwood is white and the heartwood a dull reddish-brown, with a distinct growth-ring feature.

It is straight-grained, and the texture varies from fine to coarse.

Properties
Average weight is 26 lb/ft^3. It air-dries fairly rapidly and well with little degrade, and is stable in use. It has low bending and crushing strength, low resistance to shock, very low stiffness, and a poor steam-bending rating.

Workability
Works easily with hand and machine tools, but is prone to splintering. Sharp tools are needed. It takes nails well and produces a good finish.

Preservation
It is very durable and resistant to preservative treatment.

Uses
Ideal for wooden pipes, flumes, tanks, vats, silos, and slats in water-cooling towers. Also used for caskets, interior and exterior joinery, organ pipes and much more.

4
4
7
6
6
6
H

SHOREA SPP. *FAMILY:* DIPTEROCARPACEAE

Light/Dark Red Meranti

Where it grows
A large number of species of this genus grow in south-east Asia. These timbers vary in color and density and are grouped as light red meranti, light red seraya, and white lauan; dark red meranti, dark red seraya, and red lauan.

Appearance
Details must be general because of the number of species, but the first group is pale pink to red, and in the second it is medium to dark red-brown with white resin streaks. Both have interlocked grain and a rather coarse texture.

Properties
The first group's weight averages 34 lb/ft^3, the second group 42 lb/ft^3. Drying is usually fairly rapid, without serious degrade. Both are stable in use. The first group is much weaker than the darker one. Both have medium bending and crushing strengths, low stiffness and shock resistance, and a poor steam-bending rating.

Workability
They work well with machine and hand tools, hold screws and nails satisfactorily and can be glued.

Preservation
The light group is non-durable, and the dark group is moderately durable and resistant to impregnation.

Uses
First group: interior joinery, light structural work; second group: similar, plus exterior work. Check with your local environmental group before buying.

SHOREA SPP. *FAMILY:* DIPTEROCARPACEAE

White/Yellow Meranti

shallowly interlocked grain and moderately coarse texture. The sapwood in white meranti is well defined, and the heartwood matures to a much lighter golden brown. The texture is moderately coarse.

Where it grows

The name meranti is applied to timbers from Malaya, Sarawak, and Indonesia; seraya refers to wood from Sabah.

Appearance

Yellow Meranti and Yellow Seraya sapwood is lighter in color and distinct from the heartwood, which is light yellow-brown and matures to a dull yellow-brown. They have

Properties

Yellow meranti/seraya weighs on average 30-42 lb/ft^3, while white meranti is 41 lb/ft^3. It dries slowly but well, but has a tendency to cup. It has low bending strength and shock resistance, medium crushing strength, very low stiffness, and a moderate steam-bending rating. The timbers are stable in use. White meranti/seraya dries without serious degrade, has medium strength in all categories and a very poor steam-bending rating.

Workability

Yellow meranti works satisfactorily, but the silica in white has a severe blunting effect on tools.

Preservation

They are moderately durable and the sapwood is permeable.

Uses

Both groups are used for light construction, interior joinery, furniture, and flooring. Check with your local environmental group before buying.

SWIETENIA SPP. *FAMILY:* MELIACEAE

American Mahogany

lumber. It is mostly straight-grained, and has a moderately fine to medium and uniform texture.

Where it grows

Commercial supplies come from southern Mexico, south along the Atlantic coast from Belize to Panama; in Colombia and Venezuela, Peru, Bolivia, and Brazil.

Appearance

The sapwood is yellowish-white and the heartwood varies from pale red to dark red-brown in heavier

Properties

Weighs on average 34 lb/ft^3 and can be air- or kiln-dried rapidly and well without warping or checking. It is stable in use, has low bending strength, very low stiffness and shock resistance, medium crushing strength, and a moderate steam-bending rating.

Workability

This is one of the best woods for either hand or machine tools, and sharp edges will overcome woolliness. It holds nails and screws well, glues well and gives an excellent finish.

Preservation

Liable to insect attack, this wood is durable and extremely resistant to preservative treatment.

Uses

It goes into high-class cabinets and reproduction furniture, chairs, paneling, interior joinery, domestic flooring, exterior joinery, boats, pianos, and burial caskets. Excellent for carving, engravers' blocks and engineers' patterns, molds, and dies. Produces veneer for cabinets and paneling. Check with your local environmental group before buying.

TAXUS BACCATA *FAMILY:* TAXACEAE

Yew

Where it grows
The common yew is widely distributed through Algeria, Asia Minor, the Caucasus, northern Iran, the Himalayas, and Burma, and throughout Europe.

Appearance
The heartwood varies from orange-brown streaked with darker purple, to purplish-brown with darker mauve or brown patches. It has a highly decorative appearance.

Properties
Yew is one of the heaviest of softwoods (42 lb/ft^3), and dries fairly rapidly and well with little degrade. Distortion is negligible and

it is stable in use. It has medium bending and crushing strengths, with fairly low stiffness and resistance to shock. Straight-grained, air-dried yew is one of the best softwoods for steam-bending.

Workability
Works well with hand and machine tools but tears easily when there's irregular, curly- or crossgrain. Nailing requires pre-boring.

Preservation
It is durable but not immune to attack by the common furniture beetle; it is resistant to preservative treatment.

Uses
For many years it was prized for the English archer's longbow. Now an excellent turnery and carving wood, and is used for reproduction furniture, interior and exterior joinery, garden furniture, fences, and gate posts. It is sliced for veneers.

TECTONA GRANDIS *FAMILY:* VERBENACEAE

Teak

Where it grows
Teak is indigenous to Burma and grows extensively throughout India, in Thailand, Indonesia, and Java. It has been introduced into Malaysia, Borneo, the Philippines, tropical Africa, and Central America.

Appearance
True Burma teak has a narrow, pale yellow-brown sapwood and a dark golden-brown heartwood, darkening on exposure. The grain is mostly straight in Burma teak, and wavy in Indian teak from Malabar. The texture is coarse and uneven.

Properties
Weighs 38-43 lb/ft^3, averaging 40. It dries rather slowly, and there's

small movement in service. It has medium bending strength, low stiffness and shock resistance, high crushing strength, and a moderate steam-bending classification.

Workability
Works reasonably well with hand and machine tools, and has a moderately severe blunting effect. Nailing requires pre-boring, and the wood glues and finishes well.

Preservation
The timber is very durable.

Uses
Its vast number of uses include furniture and cabinet-making, decking for ships and boats, deck houses, handrails, bulwarks,

hatches, hulls, planking, high-class joinery, and paneling. It makes very attractive flooring and laboratory benches. It is cut for all grades of plywood and veneers. Check with your local environmental group before buying.

TERMINALIA SPP. *FAMILY:* COMBRETACEAE

Indian Laurel

The grain is fairly straight to irregular and coarse-textured.

Properties
Weight averages about 53 lb/ft³, and it is a highly refractory wood to dry, prone to surface checking, warping, and splitting. It shows small movement in use, is very dense, has medium bending strength, shock resistance, and stiffness, high crushing strength, and a poor steam-bending classification.

Workability
Rather difficult to work by hand and moderately hard to machine. Difficult to nail but holds screws well and glues firmly. Needs filling for a good finish, which is best achieved with oil or wax.

Preservation
The sapwood, which is permeable, is subject to attack by the powder post beetle, but the heartwood is moderately durable and resistant to preservative treatment.

Uses
Used extensively for furniture and cabinet-making, high-class interior joinery for paneling, doors, and staircases. Excellent for turnery, and is cut for veneers. Check with your local environmental group or supplier before buying.

Where it grows
Not a true laurel, it occurs in India, West Pakistan, Bangladesh, and Burma.

Appearance
The sapwood is reddish-white and sharply defined from the heartwood, which varies from light brown with few markings to dark brown, with darker brown streaks.

⚔	6
▲	6
❖	10
▨	10
〜	6
▣	9
	H

TERMINALIA IVORENSIS *FAMILY:* COMBRETACEAE

Idigbo

Properties
Weight is variable, averaging 34 lb/ft³. It dries rapidly and well, has small movement in service, has medium density, low bending strength, very low stiffness, medium crushing strength, very low shock resistance, and a very poor steam-bending classification.

Workability
Works easily with hand and machine tools, with little dulling, but may pick up the grain on quartered surfaces. Has good screw-and nail-holding properties, glues well, takes stain readily and, when filled, provides a good finish.

Preservation
The sapwood is liable to attack by the powder post beetle and the heartwood is durable and extremely resistant to preservative treatment.

Uses
It is very useful for furniture and fine interior and exterior joinery such as window and door frames, cladding, shingles, carpentry, and building construction. Makes good domestic flooring, and is cut for plywood and veneers. Check with your local environmental group before buying.

Where it grows
It occurs in equatorial Guinea, Sierra Leone, Liberia, Ivory Coast, Ghana, and southern Nigeria.

Appearance
There's little distinction between the sapwood and heartwood, which is plain pale yellow to light pinkish-brown. Grain is straight to slightly irregular, with a medium to fairly coarse uneven texture.

⚔	2
▲	2
❖	6
▨	6
〜	4
▣	6
	H

4

4

6

6

5

6

H

TERMINALIA SUPERBA *FAMILY:* COMBRETACEAE

Afara

Where it grows
This tree occurs throughout West Africa, from the Cameroons to Sierra Leone.

Appearance
The pale yellow-brown to straw-colored heartwood is known as light afara or light limba. Heartwood with gray-black streaks is known as dark afara, dark limba, or limba bariolé, and as korina in the USA. It is straight- and close-grained, but often wavy. The texture is moderately coarse but even.

Properties
The weight is 30-40 lb/ft^3, averaging 34. This medium-density wood has low bending strength and stiffness, but medium crushing strength. Care is needed in air-drying, but kilning is rapid with little or no degrade.

Workability
Works well with hand and machine tools, but a low cutter angle is required when planing irregular grain. It glues well, provides an excellent finish when filled, and requires pre-boring before nailing or screwing.

Preservation
It is non-durable, and the sapwood is liable to attack by the powder post beetle and blue sap stain. The heartwood has moderate resistance to preservative treatment.

Uses
The light-colored wood is used in furniture and interior joinery, store and office fitting, and caskets. The darker heartwood produces very attractive face veneers for paneling and furniture, and is also good turnery wood. Check with your local environmental group or supplier before buying.

2

2

4

3

2

2

S

THUYA PLICATA *FAMILY:* CUPRESSACEAE

Western Red Cedar

Where it grows
It is known as giant abor vitae in the USA, red cedar in Canada, and British Columbia red cedar in the UK. It occurs from Alaska to south California and east from British Columbia to Washington, Idaho, Montana, and the northern Rockies.

Appearance
The sapwood is white, in contrast with the heartwood, which varies from dark chocolate in the center to salmon-pink in the outer zone. It weathers to silver-gray. It is straight-grained with a prominent growth-ring figure, and has a coarse texture and is rather brittle.

Properties
Weighs about 23 lb/ft^3. Thin sizes dry better than thick ones. There is very small shrinkage in changing atmospheres, and stability in service. It has low strength in all categories and a very poor steam-bending classification.

Workability
Works easily with hand and machine tools, with little dulling effect. Cutters should be kept very sharp. It has good nailing properties, but galvanized or copper nails should be used. It glues easily.

Preservation
Sapwood is liable to attack by the powder post beetle; the heartwood is durable and resistant to preservative treatment.

Uses
Greenhouses, sheds, beehives, exterior weatherboarding, fences.

Where it grows
This tree occurs in Sierra Leone, Nigeria, Ivory Coast, Ghana, and Liberia.

Appearance
The heartwood varies from pale blood-red to reddish-brown, and the sapwood is slightly lighter. Most is straight-grained but some logs provide a broken stripe or mottle.

TIEGHEMELLA HECKELII *FAMILY:* SAPOTACEAE

Makoré

The texture is much finer and more even than mahogany.

Properties
Average weight is 39 lb/ft³, and it dries at a moderate rate with little degrade. It shows small movement in service, has medium bending and crushing strengths, low stiffness and shock resistance, and a moderate steam-bending rating.

Workability
The silica content causes severe blunting, so carbide-tipped saws are required. Efficient dust extraction is essential. It tends to split in nailing, but takes glue well and stains and polishes to an excellent finish.

Preservation
The sapwood is liable to attack by the powder post beetle; the heartwood is very durable and extremely resistant to preservation treatment.

Uses
It is used for doors, table legs, chairs, fittings, superior interior joinery and paneling, and for exterior cladding, doors, sills and thresholds. Also used for framing for vehicles, for boats, laboratory benches, textile rollers, and turnery. Logs are cut for veneers and plywood. Check with your local environmental group or supplier before buying.

Where it grows
Several species of the lime or linden tree grow throughout Europe and eastern Asia. The closely related species *T. americana* produces basswood in Canada and the eastern USA, where it's known as American lime. *T. japonica*, Japanese lime, is known as Japanese basswood in the UK.

TILIA SPP. *FAMILY:* TILIACEAE

Lime (Basswood)

Appearance
There's no distinction between the sapwood and heartwood, which is creamy-white when the tree is felled, and matures to a pale brown. It has straight grain and a fine uniform texture, and is soft and weak.

Properties
The weight of European lime is 34 lb/ft³; American basswood and Japanese lime are 26. They dry fairly rapidly with little degrade, have medium movement in service, low to medium bending and crushing strength, low stiffness and shock resistance, and a poor steam-bending rating.

Workability
Works easily with hand and machine tools but needs thin-edged, sharp tools for a smooth finish. It nails and glues, stains and polishes, satisfactorily.

Preservation
The sapwood is prone to attack by the common furniture beetle. The heartwood is perishable but permeable to preservative treatment.

Uses
Carving, artificial limbs, beehive frames, piano sounding boards, harps; good for turnery, and is cut for veneers.

2

2

4

4

~
4

|▭|
3

H

TRIPLOCHITON SCLEROXYLON *FAMILY:* TRIPOLOCHITONACEAE

Obeche

Where it grows
It occurs throughout West Africa.

Appearance
There's little distinction between the sapwood and heartwood, which is creamy-yellow to pale straw-colored. The grain is interlocked, producing a striped appearance on quartered stock, and the texture is moderately coarse but even. The wood has a natural luster.

Properties
Weighs about 24 lb/ft^3, and dries very rapidly with no tendency to split, but slight distortion may occur. It exhibits small movement in service, has low bending and crushing strengths, very low stiffness and shock resistance, and a moderate to poor steam-bending rating.

Workability
Works easily with both hand and machine tools, with only slight blunting. Sharp cutters with a reduced angle are recommended. It nails easily but has poor holding qualities. Glues well, but needs a light grain filling before finishing.

Preservation
This non-durable wood tends to stain blue if in contact with iron compounds in moist conditions. The sapwood is liable to attack by the powder post beetle. Heartwood is perishable and resistant to preservative treatment, and the sapwood is permeable.

Uses
Whitewood furniture and fitments, interior rails, drawer slides and linings, cabinet framing, interior joinery and the like. Check with your local environmental group before buying.

4

▲
4

❖
5

4

~
6

|▭|
6

S

TSUGA HETEROPHYLLA *FAMILY:* PINACEAE

Western Hemlock

Where it grows
This softwood tree occurs in Alaska, British Columbia, northern Washington, Idaho, and the western slopes of the Cascades. It has also been planted in Britain. It is known as Pacific hemlock and British Columbian hemlock in the USA.

Appearance
The heartwood is cream with a pale brown cast. It is straight-grained with a fairly even texture and is somewhat lustrous.

Properties
It weighs 30 lb/ft^3 and needs careful drying. Distortion is minimal, there is little movement in service. The wood has medium bending and crushing strengths, low hardness and stiffness, and a moderate steam-bending rating.

Workability
It works readily with hand and machine tools with little dulling. Can be glued, stained, painted or varnished with a good finish, but should be pre-bored for nailing near the ends of dry boards.

Preservation
Damage by *Siricid* wood wasps is sometimes present. Sapwood may be liable to attack by the common furniture beetle. The wood is non-durable and is not resistant to decay. The heartwood is resistant to preservative treatment.

Uses
Building, joists, rafters, interior and exterior joinery; good for turnery; logs are cut for veneers and plywood.

ULMUS SPP. *FAMILY:* ULMACEAE

European Elm

Where it grows
These species occur widely throughout the temperate climes of Europe, western Asia, North America, and Japan. They are known by many names.

Appearance
The heartwood is usually a dull brown, often with a reddish tint, and is clearly defined from the paler sapwood by having distinct and irregular growth rings, giving it a rather coarse texture. It is crossgrained and of irregular growth, providing an attractive figure. Mainland European elms tend to be more straight-grained.

Properties
European and Japanese elms weigh about 34 lb/ft^3, wych elm about 42 lb/ft^3. It dries fairly rapidly with a tendency to distort. It has low bending and crushing strengths, with very low stiffness and resistance to shock. All elms have a good steam-bending rating.

Workability
Can be difficult to work, tending to pick up in planing and bind on the saw, but takes nails well, glues satisfactorily and provides a good finish.

Preservation
The permeable sapwood is liable to attack by the powder post beetle and common furniture beetle. It is non-durable and moderately resistant to preservative treatment.

Uses
Marine work, gym equipment, implements, vehicle bodywork; good for flooring; is sliced for veneers.

ULMUS THOMASII *FAMILY:* ULMACEAE

American Elm

Where it grows
There are five species of the *Ulmus* genus growing in eastern Canada and the USA. White elm is produced in eastern Canada and central parts of the USA (it is also known as water elm, swamp elm, and American elm). There are also slippery elm and rock elm.

Appearance
The heartwood is medium to light reddish-brown and the sapwood slightly paler. Rock elm is straight-grained with a moderately fine texture. White elm is sometimes interlocked and the texture coarse and woolly.

Properties
White elm weighs 36 lb/ft^3, slippery elm is a little heavier, while rock elm weighs 39-49 lb/ft^3 . The wood dries readily. American elms have medium bending and crushing strengths and very low stiffness. White elm has high resistance and rock elm very high resistance to shock. All have very good steam-bending ratings.

Workability
They work fairly easily with only moderate blunting, take nails, glue easily and provide a good finish.

Preservation
Sapwood is prone to the powder post beetle, but resistant to fungus. Elm is non-durable and moderately resistant to preservative.

Uses
Boats and ships, other marine use, ice hockey sticks; gym equipment; veneers.

INDEX OF COMMON NAMES